Laugh at the End of the World

Laugh at the End of the World

Collected Comic Poems 1969-1999

Bill Knott

BOA Editions, Ltd. ❧ Rochester, NY ❧ 2000

LC #: 99–85899
ISBN: 1–880238–84–5 A paperback original

First Edition
00 01 02 03   7 6 5 4 3 2 1

Some of the poems in this book appeared previously in
Poems: 1963 -1988 (University of Pittsburgh Press, 1989)

Publications by BOA Editions, Ltd.—
a not-for-profit corporation under section 501 (c) (3)
of the United States Internal Revenue Code—
are made possible with the assistance of grants from
the Literature Program of the New York State Council on the Arts,
the Literature Program of the National Endowment for the Arts,
the Lannan Foundation, the Sonia Raiziss Giop Charitable Foundation,
the Eric Mathieu King Fund of The Academy of American Poets,
The Halcyon Hill Foundation, as well as from
the Mary S. Mulligan Charitable Trust, the County of Monroe, NY,
Towers Perrin, and from many individual supporters.

*   *   *

See Colophon Page
for Acknowledgement of Special Individual Supporters.

Cover Design: Daphne Poulin-Stofer
Typesetting: Richard Foerster
Manufacturing: McNaughton & Gunn, Lithographers
BOA Logo: Mirko

BOA Editions, Ltd.
Steven Huff, Publisher
Richard Garth, Chair, Board of Directors
A. Poulin, Jr., President & Founder (1976–1996)
260 East Avenue
Rochester, NY 14604

www.boaeditions.org

"... it all seemed so strangely funny that I laughed until the tears came. I suddenly wondered if the phrase, 'the great laugh at the end of the world,' that occurs in one of my husband's poems, didn't mean something . . ."

—Osamu Dazai, from *Villon's Wife*
(translated by Donald Keene)

The order of the poems is random, neither thematic nor chronological.

THE MAN WHO MARRIED HIS CHECKOUT LANE

Daily, in the supermarket where I go,
I gravitate to this one lane—the one
that's most full—you know: the busiest one.
Have I fallen in love with my checkout lane?

Well, I am male, I feel drawn to this aisle;
its openness is shameless, selfishly exciting;
the real way it squeezes my shoppingcart
and deigns to crowd me in. Oh my checkout lane

has the longest wait of any—though unlike
all these others in line, I won't leaf through the life
those tabloids provide rumors of: none of them

are beautiful as what infills me as I enter
as I am queued up for that brief orgasm
as my cash is on the counter and I am free.

ADULTERER WITH NO MOUTH AMUSES WORLD*

Not having a mouth is no joke! Imagine an ax
left by somebody, sinksank into some treetrunk:
and each day you go by, the embedded ax seems
higher, higher, until finally, one day, jumping,
you're just barely able to brush the fine of the
grain of the bottom of the axhandle with your
fingertips—and yet the tree has not grown. Nor
have you shrunk. Imagine: imagine trying to
explain this to someone if you didn't have a mouth.

* Newspaper misprint

SONG OF BRASÍLIA

From city to city
We trailed at our heels
Smiling like a suitcase
Through the passport reels
And wasn't it
Good to find a new town
With a new round
Of stars and bars and fabulous
Stays in hotel towers
Wasn't it good to have a slow one
And hour away the hours with a glow on
And when the blush was off we could just cough
And say Well it's time to go on
We could just doff our hats
And say Sorry but I've got to catch
The next wind that's blowing

But alas
This is the last
City on old earth
We'll have to stay here until
A newer one is built

We had combed Kansas City long ago
And Bangkok was old-hat
And oh gosh Paris we can only bear
Just before or just after a guerre
Yes for us the streets were no longer rolled out
We shuddered no matter what the conductor called out
We yawned in fear
We had been everywhere that's anywhere
On this old map
Then one day we were told that
In the middle of Brazil
Completely surrounded by jungle

Is the place to which we could travel
A brand new city was beginning to be built
Yes a giant new city was being mowed out
Of the jungle
And we were saved

But all too fast
This has become the last
City on our planet
And we're trapped down here until
A newer one is somewhere built

Each day we scour the papers for skyscrapers and their kind
And we try not to think of the precincts we left behind
Cause every true traveler knows
You can't go back to those
Places you've already been
No you can't go back to them

Now this is the last city
We'll see
But one
And we'll rot down here until
The devil
Gives us the key
To that town

ADVICE FROM THE EXPERTS

I lay down in the empty street and parked
My feet against the gutter's curb while from
The building above a bunch of gawkers perched
Along its ledges urged me don't, don't jump.

MOVIE-Q'S

*

Ben Lyons was typically blunt
in *I Cover the Waterfront*—
his cute co-star Claudette Colbert
could have frenched it: 'Ze waterfront, I co-vair.'

*

Attack of the 50 Foot Woman
is not a film appeals to everyone—
but I, I like the way it feels, I guess,
to have a whole town look up my dress.

*

Although by gorgeous Gene Tierney
he was loved, and loved sincerely,
Richard Widmark proved pretty shitty.
The flick? *Night and the City*.

*

*Those Incredibly Strange Creatures Who
Stopped Living and Became Mixed-up Zombies* blew
my mind, man. Like wow! (—Was I crazy? Was I sick?
Maybe I shouldn't have watched it through that Thai-stick.)

*

I know Jack Nicholson played a cameo—
and Elton John played a song or so—
and Ann-Margaret played his mommy—
but *who* the hell else was in *Tommy*?

*

It's a crime shame that that scene where
Sean Penn tied you know Madonna to a chair
and then put on her dress and licked her thighs
got like totally cut out of *Shanghai Surprise*.

*

How many of you gazeekoids went yumyum
Watching that transmutated geek Jeff Goldblum
Rip off his own ear and eat it? *The Fly* was great!
(And if he'd unzipped his fly, ripped *that* off, and ate?)

Note: I don't know if the Movie-Q constitutes a form per se, but I made up some
rules for it: the complete name of the film must appear in a quatrain rhymed
AABB. The Movie-Q must try to be funny, or piquant, or pointed. Etc., etc.,
though actually I can't think of any more rules.

TO MY PLANETARY CO-OCCUPANTS

How would you prefer to meet your fate—
by Nature or Culture?

(Nature: snakebites lightningstrikes cliffslides etc.)
(Culture: nukebreaks pesticidisms ethniccleansings etc.)

—If an alligator swallowed you
would you consider that demise purer

than if freedom fighters blew up
your commuter flight?

Or would you go vindicated re your belief in
human sovereignty

when a virus broadcast by the the CIA
got you (maybe it already has)—

If it were up to me, I would take
centuries/eons in deciding this question,

but since it isn't, since it's a question of since,
and since the number of options in

the category of Nature
seem to be getting extincter and extincter,

I ask you again to choose—
In fact, I beg you to make your choice

and make it quickly,
especially if it is to die via me.

THE RUINS-READER

I-beams uphold that wall—
You-beams bolster me: guess
Which one is going to fall.

UNSPEAKABLE

A comma is a period which leaks.

MY FAVORITE WORD

"Attentionspan" is my favorite word
because I can never finish
reading it all the way through.

FRAMEPOEM

First, make a 100 minute movie. Then take the 1
million 440 thousand frames, or stills: take each
frame, blow it up, print it, put a frame around it,
then take all 1 million 440 thousand pictures, hang
them in a gallery, consecutively in a line so that
the first frame of the movie is the first picture
inside the door and the last, last: you get the
idea. Then have the people who come in RUN past
the 1 million 440 thousand pictures, so that in
this way they become both spectator and projector.

SONG

When my shadow falls off of me
I yell "So long!"
But when I fall off my shadow
It cries "Long so!"

It seems obvious
That one of us
Is either falling wrong
Or calling wrong.

DEATH AND THE MOUNTAIN

> "There is no theme for old age
> but death and the mountain."
> —Arab proverb

You should see the treeline on
that mountain
of update bulletin news;
no avalanche can blacklist me—
The twigline on the tree
said: You should see him on talkshows

sandpapering his
mug off totempoles, carved
of old, of pine—
Just past the christline
on that cross is
one sitcom one summit of this; scarred

as a skyline of thorns it grew
up, imperious, pious. . . . To
blindfold the precipice
before leaping
from it, okay; but try keeping
a straight face

when the punchline comes "kersplat"—
There, old skin-quilt,
saint peacock hedge! Feverchart
that wedges the door shut.
I see it
he said. I see my mountain's peak-sized fate.

BEDDYBYE

Just hope that when you lie down your toes are a firing-squad

3 A.M.

Time to pare down, pull in, simplify;
—I'll buy a dark coat, move my lips when I read
the bestseller lists. . . .

ANOTHER COLD WAR POEM

So what if you lived only
One second longer
Than we
Did: to us
You will always be known as the Survivor.

AT THE MUSEUM THIS WEEK

Poland Through The Centuries a touring
Exhibition of maps drawn
By German and Russian cartographers reveals
There never was a Poland.

MYOPIA

I know that blinking lubricates
the sight and keeps it safe—
but did this World-Eye really
need the lid of my brief life?

ESCAPE PLAN

I examine
my skin

searching for
the pore

with EXIT
over it

THE DAILY ROUNDS

I keep a TV monitor on my chest
so that all who approach me
can see themselves
and respond appropriately.

QUICKIE

Poetry
is
like
sex
on
quicksand
viz
foreplay
should
be
kept
at
a
minimum

MORE USELESS ENVY

When I imagine the cameras of fame
homing in on me for a closeup,
I back away, my back pressed against
my eyes nose mouth: the reign of the same.

Failure has surrounded me with flesh,
with human-remaining-human features—
Which is no consolation—Which does
not make up for all the psychic scars

those glitter-gifted faces inflict upon
the crowd wherein I'm crammed
trying to be as inconspicuous as I am!

Daily I watch the famous zoom past.
God, I wish I could persuade some void
to synopsize its emptiness with this.

EN PASSANT

While orbiting
the earth
at a height of one millimeter
I notice
it tickles.

FEEDING THE SUN

One day we notice that the sun
needs feeding. Immediately
a crash programs begins: we fill
rockets with wheat, smoke-rings,
razorblades, then, after long aiming
—they're off. Hulls specially alloyed
so as not to melt before the stuff
gets delivered we pour cattle rivers
windmills, aborigines etcet into the sun
which however, grows stubbornly
smaller, paler. Finally of course
we run out of things to feed the thing,
start shipping ourselves. By now
all the planets-moons-asteroids and
so on have been shoveled in though
they're not doing much good it's still
looking pretty weak, heck, nothing helps!
Now the last few of us left lift off.
The trip seems forever but then, touchdown.
Just before entering we wonder,
will we be enough. There's a last-second
doubt in our minds: can we, can this
final sacrifice, our broughten crumb,
satiate it—will a glutteral belch burst
out then at last,—and will that Big Burp

be seen by far-off telescopes, interpreted
as a nova by those other galaxies,
those further stars which have always
seemed even more starving than ours?

THE PATRIOTS

at the edge of the city in
the garbagedump where the
trucks never stop unloading
a crazy congregation stumbles
from trashmound to trashheap
they smash their fists down on
whatever's intact they tear
to bits the pitifew items
that have remained whole they
rip everything old clothes
papers cans bones to nothing
with their glazed teeth
the enlightened the faithful
every few meters one of them
falls and is torn to shreds by
the others at the edge of
the city where there's a line
waiting to join

SUMMER ACTION FEATURES

Can I kiss this cinema's utter pittedness.

Moviescreen, you hype of hygiene, I love
to see a face lace its venom with mine.

When the hero has far too many minotaur scars,
the creases in my palms turn over and nap.

Archimedes revised: if I sink far enough
into the film, the law of displacement
should bring to the surface my truest self.

Then the blow-ups come on cue. The ingenue
glows like the sky: we both gnaw raw halo.

God knows I know each bomb is a mobile
some sculptor has failed ineptly to keep aloft.

Even I am losing my innocent twitter balance,
though statistically I will die eating purse soup.

PRISCILLA, *or* THE MARVELS OF ENGINEERING

(A Fatal Fable)

A "Swingles Only" Cruise to souths tour on the
S.S. Priscilla: parties, spurtive romances, confided
Antiperspirants, quickchange partners. Suddenly
3rd day poolside blank, sun
Ouch I meet up a daze dish somehow ain't
Crossed my eyes' equator yet: she preened
To have appeared out of that presumptuous

Nowhere our hoarse soggy captain's
Nailed in place on his compass: in all the swarmy sticky
Nightlong pairings off, secret lifeboat
Drill assignations, where did you come from
I offered haven't laid uh eyes you behind musta been blind. Oh
I've been around she said, I've seen you operating
That blonde last night, har, har, har.
Flattered, I introduced my name's Bill. Priscilla.
—As in S.S.? We laughed over the coincidence,
Wringing fragile martini chill stems all
Around us similar neo couples were
Gangplanking each other, coral lounge dusk deck.
Dinner, we promised. Then the moviedance,
Then . . . ? Our eyebrows guessed "The night?"
Separating to change, we hugged all sprinkly
But at table that P.M. I stained her napkin but
She didn't show up went looking for wasn't at the dance
Either. Hmmpf, not on deck—where could she
Be? I asked all the other cats and chicks
Where the hell's Priscilla? describing her. No way
Man ain't never seen no piece like that since we
Ask the purser—man you sure? Tete
A tete sure, I replied. The purser!
I'll get her cabin number, she might not be feeling
Oh boy I didn't inadvertantly slip a torpedo into her drink that
Stud I scored from said they work every,
The purser. But no senor
There is no Priscilla everywhere listed amongs
The passenger list I'm jorry. The boat—she
Is S.S. Priscilla? he added helpfully, concerned, as though I were
    nutlong no
No you nit-tit—she has to be on look I met her this
Safternoon in the "Cock 'N' Tail" Lounge. Jorry
Is no let me have that thing here on the passenger look for jourselve.
Damn! she ain't on it
A stowaway hunh

That's even better
I'LL get her
She can't escape what's
Gonna do—hide in the ocean?
But
Finally, frustrato, angry not even drunk after no
Go searching all night, at sailor's-dawn I slunk to my cabin and
Guess who I found the bitch all tucked up in that little cute-ass
Type beds they have Priscilla!
I hissed. Come to bunk
She swelled. But you, you aren't . . .
Aren't what, know whatcha 're crazy dam-
Shh let's love she swayed. Okay: I'm game. 'S bout time. So we
Start fucking but, her movements were too calm
And rocking, elusive as chase in tune with the ship's
Wash on the waves. Gentle, coaxing, mocking-
Musky, chromosome zoney, internal
As sea. It was eeeerie
The ex of it cited
Frightened me. My Y shot up: I began
Fug and fury ramming, I urged
Harsh thrash strokes, I hard
To hurt her with my penis, I remembered
That Norman Mailer story where he calls his "The
Avenger" I was pissed, make me
Frantic look all over the goddamn
Ship you cunt slammed all my spite ptooey
Into her. And then, and then . . . instantly . . .
Something . . . all I know is I came the split
I hit the water. I was drowned, of course,
In the famous shipwreck. The famous shipwreck
You remember
It was in all the TV—
Shots of it sunk in shallow clear just
Off an atoll. And everyone aboard was lost, adios,
Unusual or not unusual in these cases. But no one
Nobody could figure out how

The S.S. Whatshername had
Gotten all those great big gaping holes
Ripped, slashed, torn in her hull nor
What caused this deadfall rupture, the grievous eely capsizing.

Couldn't a been a iceberg
That
      far
          south.

BRIGHTON ROCK BY GRAHAM GREENE

Pinky Brown must marry Rose Wilson
to keep her mouth shut about the murder
which the cops don't know wasn't no accident—

Pinky has a straight razor for slashing,
a vial of acid for throwing into,
a snitch's face. He dies in the end. The end

of the book, I mean—where, on the last page,
'Young Rose' hurries out of church to pray
that her Pinky has left her preggy-poo . . .

Now, this kid—if he was ever born—joined
a skiffle group in '62 called Brighton
Rockers, didn't make it big, though,

just local dances and do's. Rose,
pink, brown, all nonelemental colors, shades
of shame, melancholy, colors which, you

get caught loving too much, you get sent up
to do time—time, that crime you didn't,
couldn't commit! even if you weren't

born—even and if your dad he died with
that sneer—unsmooched his punk's pure soul, unsaved—
Every Sunday now in church Rose slices

her ring-finger off, onto the collection-plate;
once the sextons have gathered enough
bodily parts from the congregation, enough

to add up to an entire being, the priest sub-
stitutes that entire being for the one
on the cross: they bring Him down in the name

of brown and rose and pink, sadness
and shame, His body, remade, is yelled at
and made to get a haircut, go to school,

study, to do each day like the rest
of us crawling through this igloo of hell,
and laugh it up, show pain a good time,

and read Brighton Rock by Graham Greene.

CRAPSHOOT

Whoever it was, the first plagiarist
had to actually dream up the concept
of the crime, so don't fault him (I imagine
this culprit as male, but the poem he copped
was—I would bet—authored by a woman)
for lack of originality. I wish

I could excuse his bad act as madness—
that a crazy theory whose tenets value
words over typos caused him to go true,
to trace out hers so unerringly—
instead of greed, I'd plead psychosis
and cry, He's Realism's victim: that's why

his poor misled hand tried to break those laws
which make omnipresent subatomic flaws
subvert the verb of every medium
and blur our sheerest copier's laserbeam:
say now his felony should be absolved, since
wise Heisenberg has found that once and once

only can the poem stay per se, regardless
of Benjamin's *Das Kunstwerk im Zeitalter
seiner technischen Reproduzierbarkeit:*
why couldn't I call his vile counterfeits
brave attempts, brilliant schemes to outmaneuver
the ways physics limits our digits' genius?

I wish I could. But, I can't. No: he's to blame—
just him, I think. Yes: the wank-ink of his name
on her work is un- , un- , un- , is a sin
I must atone. Oh, if he had only cloned
her signature the same as her poem,
no harm would have come from his plagiarism!

I write this knowing that random quantum
impurities in the surface body
of the paper or scanscreen on which
this is printed will betray all I say
here to some degree, any is too much—
each thought emits a glitch, thought Mallarmé.

I pray this page permits perfect access
what I would guess my xerox intended

to be a sincere apology to Ms.
Sappho and her sis, but may indeed instead
(despite our dearest efforts) appear as
the very opposite of what you've read.

LOVE, HATE, LIFE, DEATH, MAMA, WATER, ETC.

If everyone on this planet was forced to write
one word on a piece of paper, their favorite

word, the resulting anthology might add up to less
than Shakespeare, who had, or so I've read,

a 40K vocabulary: wouldn't most of us
just put down the same few words; how many could

avoid the usual abstract homilars, our limited
minds consisting of each other, non sequitur. I would

be ashamed to show that book to my UFO guests,
no matter how repeated or urgent their requests.

WART-HOUND

Not even those pirate's teethmarks on the moon
can tell the real as opposed to the false gold,
which is why the welcome mat nailed across
my mirror needs dusting. What's the use—

Because if I opt for the truth as opposed
to the tooth that slashed those obviously

painful crateratrices on the moon, I too
am one the drossiness of fate lacerates—

Which is why all I do now is I hang around
barbershops, scouring the floor with catchcanny eye
in search of a wart that's suffered similarly:

Fallen wart, comrade, hacked off by haste or
the CIA, hey wart, whoa wart. Here you go,
wartypoo, into this test-tube with you.

TREASON

Do our footsteps really want to become footprints?—
I mean: think of snails—if
one of them could move as fast as one of us—

wouldn't he be a traitor to his own—
a turncoat—a 'turn-snail'—?
No, no! Please don't pick them up and throw them;
they can't fly. They can only move

as they move, oh so endlessly across
this same ground we walk across ourselves
quite easily, not even hurrying:
this oh so same ground covered

with our foolish, wastrelly footprints—
which will never, never become footsteps!
(But see how quickly I become a turn-human.)

SHAME

In the whole universe I alone
Was unable to soften the impact,
Cushion the recoil of the M-16
Upon the M-17's shoulder.

HISTORY

Hope . . . goosestep.

THROWBACKS

I want to take your place in my life so
I lie in wait for you everywhere. Once I used
To lie down in the paths of steamrollers, my teardrops
Were photographed at the feet of glaciers
To prove if they were advancing or retreating
Like positions in a kama sutra: after the cold
Juggernauts passed over I was fed lingeringly
Through printer-outers. It was read then that the
E-pore is used most frequently by my skin,
Next came x, p, o . . .

I want you to take my place in my life so
I follow you everywhere. Once I used
To follow burglars around: waiting at the window till
They ransacked a house then fled, I'd enter
Run my hands through its emptied drawers, degleamed
Jewelboxes, my sole thrill was to rub the feel
Of deceived receptacles, rifled pockets.
I'd wait outside, then rush in, clambering like an adam's apple.

I want to take my place in your life so
I go with you everywhere. Once I used
To accompany myself, I had a passport to the xerox,
The unanimous aimed its initials at me on the run,
When I died my clones were laid out at the funeral
Beside me, then a heckler who's amnesiac, anybody, some
Forever stranger was blindfolded and led past the coffins to
See if they could get the right I by feel but failed
And so their life was took in place, and so I took your life
As place, so I must now keep placing your life in take,

In sudden give and take:
I want you to take my place in your life. Please.

BARREN PRECINCT

(homage Hagiwara Sakutaro)

Tightropes cross swayingly from church belfry
to church belfry, in one street a pileup of mattresses
is burning. If it were snowing it would be
like their very first sheets returning,
fresh from the sky's laundry. In the bracingly cold air
I see doorframes with no houses, houses with no rooms, and houses
where they serve lunch in its most naive form. I amble toward
a wood fence, a childishly-chalked bullseye, in which
I find some kind of old military medal pinned dead center:
the metal has a pale, harmful ribbon; it flutters and or rattles whitely,
    whitely withstanding the wind,
defending the bullseye's secret, inmost ring.
If cornered, I would agree—with almost no argument—:
this medal should get a medal!

Barren precinct,
eyes stare at you without our even knowing,
like the statue of a buddha
they regard you with immobilized eyes, with
carven idol eyelids,
you are the eternal non-unguent of tearless eyes,
the blink that will never be.

Note:
Hiroaki Sato's translation of Hagiwara's "A Barren Area" inspired this poem—
which means I borrowed its subject and mood, but not its content. It's an hom-
age, not an adaptation. Also, it's an attempt at *hon'yaku-cho*, a favorite mode of
Hagiwara, according to Sato, who defines it as "Translation style . . . writings
that read like clumsy translations."
Line 1: "J'ai tendu des cordes de clocher à clocher . . ." —Rimbaud.

BEACHED

Thaw, summer, melt from pastel to pastille—
a fruit's sweetness warning the greatness of death
to back off: hornbeeps, skidmarks so new, so fresh.

Cars, go and surround each beach.
Where drowned armpits flower toward the word.
Where even the sun refuses to be an icon.

In my room stand two razorpoles. I rub
back and forth between them. I vacillate
love, hate: it's exhausting continually

wiping the spittle off your face,
though the spitting itself is of course
quite effortless. Simile for waves.

GOLLY MOUNTAIN BLUES

Up on Golly Mountain all the lovers are parked
Wish we could be up there enjoyin the dark
But you don't wanna I'm sorry I come along
Cause you won't stop the car hon all night long
> Hairpin turns up and down the mountainside
> Hairpin turns drivin like a suicide
> I know you ain't to blame but
> Our love's about to flame out
> Can't you smell the rubber burn
> As you keep riding them hairpin turns
When you told me you loved danger I said then I'm your guy [girl]
I been dangerous since I first learned to kiss
Let's go up on Golly and give it a try [whirl]
But when I said I loved it I sure didn't mean this
> Hairpin turns up and down the mountainside
> Hairpin turns drivin like a suicide
> I can't remember your name but
> Our love's about to flame out
> Can't you feel the floorboards burn
> As you keep riding them hairpin turns
I heard about some funny ways that people get their kicks
From runnin round upon the town to gettin hit with whips
But you take the cake my friend you're oddball number one
I admire your nerves but I got some curves where you could have
  more fun than these here
> Hairpin turns up and down the mountainside
> Hairpin turns drivin like a suicide
> I guess it's all the same but
> Our love's about to flame out
> Can't you taste the seat of my bluejeans burn
> As you keep riding them hairpin turns
Poor baby I know it ain't your fault it was your mama daddy they
musta dropped you on your brake when you was born cause if you
don't know that lovin is the deadliest thrill there is you don't know
nothin I shoulda known somethin when you picked me up inside the

movieshow way your windshield wiper kept gettin into my popcorn
here let me take these hairpins outa my hair and let it fall into your
lap don't that make you want to love me and cuddle and lay your
head on my soft soft shoulder . . . Soft Shoulder? Hey! Look out!
> Hairpin turns up and down the mountainside
> Hairpin turns drivin like a suicide
> It's a dirty shame but
> Our love's about to flame out
> Can't you tell my poor heart yearns
> But you just keep on riding them hairpin turns
> Yes you just keep on riding them
> > hair-
> > > pin—
Get your tongue off that gaspedal baby
You tryin to love this thing or drive it well then drive it drive it
Just cause you ain't got nothin to live for . . . heck, come to think of
  it I ain't got nothin neither
Hey you know somethin? I'm beginning to like it
> Hairpin turns up and down the mountainside
> Hairpin turns drivin like a suicide
> I know you ain't to blame but
> Our love's about to flame out
> Can't you smell the rubber burn
> As you keep riding them hairpin turns

FUNNY POEM

death loves rich people
more than us poor
coffin salesmen look down their sniffs
shoot their cuffs
at us

funeral directors obit-pages priests
all want classy
can't afford
a headstone
a silk lining
daily lawn mowers flowers plus
catering service for the worms
they act mortally insulted

and you know it's funny
while I never
believed that stuff about god
loving
the poor so much
made so many

I never believed that stuff about god
but this
death preferring the rich thing you know
it's kind of funny but you know
I believe it
it makes sense

in fact
I think we
should start a movement
our slogan would be
GIVE DEATH WHAT IT WANTS

yes
let's lend it a helpin' hand
be neighborly
it makes sense
since what death seems to want is
the dead
i.e. the rich

AT THE CROSSROADS

The wind blows a piece of paper to my feet.

I pick it up.

It is not a petition for my death.

PASTIME

surreptitious
and mute
are the vendors of my beauty

hide and seek
hucksters their
occupation pointless
as the toss

of playing cards into
a hat that's simultaneously
being thrown into a halo on
the fly so to speak

though I know
I'm supposed to say
on the wing

UNREDEEMED

Whimsical god, the window
Smites me then heals me, smites—
Blindness, sight, blindness, sight.

Its slats open-and-close like
A xerox tendering
ECT to Saul click Paul

Click Saul again. Identity
Steps from past, from presto,
Over the naked thresh of

Whose hold on my flesh. Oh yes,
I know, I should live in shun—
Hibernate against my soul, and

Eat sandal snow: why must I go
Forth of this house to meet
To market, to take my part

At that crossplace of values
A daily pilgrim, debt-devout—
Why does my heart in its gut

Obedient need to carry out
Every Outremerican's
Highest, most sacred duty:

To shop. Hey, it fills a gap,
This superstitious shlep
From store to store, without stop

(And yet prophets pray that one day
I'll never have to leave my mind
But via Internet will find

Virtual all these bargains)—
Pure-plus ritual! as though
Buying this or buying that

Could keep me whole: old hymnal
Of dollars cents, dear virgo
Intacta whose observance

By true consumerism gains
Through worship a kind of
Tithe-sustained sanity—

In fact, to quote our President,
Mental health is normed-in
To it—proportionate, shared—

There's a slice for each of us—
In fact, it's a communion:
This holy, wholesome vision

Is how we creamed the Commies
And saved our ass, not to mention
Mom's apple pie pietà,

The caesarean of which
Might (misfortunately)
Render me unto me. So when—

When ATM time comes
I too shall face the humbling flash
Screen of that machine designed

To scan in half the once sans self
And watch it flick its widget slots
Deigning to bless even

A wretch as worthless as this:
But when, according to the stats
In the Bible, Arcturus

Bi-millennially aligns
With the intransigence of
Human transactions, its

Bank of blinks, its solstice vault
Promising to spill out
Flushing our customer sills with

What, another Nativity,
I will not insert my KashKard
Or enter, while the Mall

Dies around me, my personal
Passcode word, my number ID—
I'll ram in, not plastic, but

(Begatitude-foretold)
My aura's errata, my
Freud's flaws. Although only

(*Saith says*) the clone can, the mote's
Eye may, et cetera. In fact,
Such acts of heresy would cost

More gold than I could bear
The loss. And so, therefore, ergo—
Duly each dawn I rise, I raise

The blinds and nail my shoulders
To a t-square, let light strip
To my skin, a birthgraft,

A natal fate. And so, and so—
I manage a moue or two;
I make, like, acknowledgement.

Note:
2 of the possible epigraphs for this poem:

"Bush to Xmas Shoppers: Spend, Spend, Spend!
Economy Reborn, Prez Says"
—Newspapers, Nov–Dec 1991

"It seems to me that the individual today stands at a crossroads, faced with the choice of whether to pursue the existence of a blind consumer, subject to the implacable march of new technology and the endless multiplication of material goods, or to seek out a way that would lead to spiritual responsibility, a way that ultimately might mean not only his personal salvation but also the saving of society at large; in other words, to turn to God. He has to resolve this dilemma for himself, for only he can discover his own sane spiritual life."
—Andrey Tarkovsky, *Sculpting in Time* (1986)

PENNY WISE

well alright
I grant you
he was a fascist
ahem antisemitism the
er war and all
I'm not defending them
but at least
you've got to admit
at least he
made the quatrains run on time

Note:
2 puns explain the title and last line: "Penny wise, pound foolish"—
And: Mussolini's admirers used to say, "Well, he may be a fascist, but at least he makes the trains run on time."

FIRST

No sooner has the lightningbolt struck earth
than a snake encurls itself around it.
Ah, rhyme-me, if my metaphors
could only pounce like that.

The male form is still recognizable
until you get about halfway down.
Then one notices the scrotum
more than masticating a stick of gum!

Like a halo slanted to catch the last
rays of a hair, I hold up my life
determined to sound some farfinitesimal thing.

Why, whenever a bird pecks out the suits
from a deck of cards, does it do hearts first?
Heck, why not peck out my penis first?

RITUAL

first
bury your hands
then the third from the right toes
your pancreas bury it next
and so on in the order prescribed
by ancient strictures
save the head for last
cup your thumbs beneath for it to fall into
have an eyelash
be the last thing visible overground
leave a heartbeat
to tamp down the dirt
to be a shadow for grassblade above

then nothing up there
at the beginning of this poem nothing
so that the last the very last
all that'll be left to do then is
bury your hands
etc.

HUMAN ESCAPE SYNDROME

Often our pendulum-curtained ocean
was thought to harbor a metronome,
which saddled the minutehand
and rode off to catch the hourhand.

Time's simile? Waves. Waves—teeter empires,
primed to fall, defined to fall.
But now time is digital.

Now time has no time for metaphors;
a cyborg is not a mime of me.
Human: android with a lobotomy.

I climb the cliff above time's sea.
The steep—and pull myself up by a thread
that dangles from the sutures,
one of the sutures in my forehead.

POEM NOIR

(Braille Balls)
Angry at my wife I drove out to our
Cottage by the lake. Around 1 AM a March shower
Began to fall and when I went out on the porch

To see it I saw a young man lurch
Into the lake with all his clothes on. There
Was nobody else around, the other cottages were
Dark, as was mine. He kept walking straight out
And soon the water was over his head. I shout-
Ed but he obviously didn't hear. He was trying
To drown himself! So I swam out and grabbed him. Sighing,
I resuscitated him. He lay on our bed
Smiling. Thanks a lot but no thanks, he said.
Then he convinced me that no matter what I did
He was going to commit suicide.
I had an idea: Does it make any difference how
You do it? I asked him. No, he replied,
What do you mean. Well, what about the electric

(I Want My Friends In Woody Lots, With French Toast Up Their
    Nostrils)
Chair? Would you care if it was that? No,
He said. Well I'll send ten thousand dollars
To anyone you cite, if you'll kill my wife and
Go to the electric chair for it. Yes,
He said, I'll pretend to be a burglar, kill her, then get
Caught. Send the ten grand to N, who rejected me. She'll
Feel sorrier then when I'm dead. He grinned. I
Said, Great. The next night I slipped
My wife 2 sleeping-pills then drove to my brother's
To try to establish an alibi but he got drunk,
Passed out so that was no go—damn.
When I got home I went right to my wife's room where
I found her snoring. What the hell, I said. Then
The phone rang. It was my brother,
He said someone had murdered our father. Father!
I said. A hectic day followed. Police, the tax
Lawyers, not to mention, my worthless alibi.
Finally that night I sat up late waiting for the guy

(Eel-tripled Eyes and Freezing Initials)
Who was supposed to murder my wife. The phone rang. My
Brother had been killed! I was chief suspect
Since I inherited the family millions. Wake up, wake up,
I shook my wife, but the 3 sleeping-pills etcetera.
The police followed me all the next day
But I slipped them. They didn't know I was hitting all the joints
To try and find that young drown man. We
Had a few things to discuss: That night
Down by the deserted docks we fought.
I was slugged into the river and I drowned.
No-one ever saw him. When they found
My body the coroner ruled suicide over remorse at my terrible
    crimes.
He had done the murders but I got the blame.
My wife got all the money, and married him.

TRIP

. . . Jesus walking on the water
. . . keeps tripping over
. . . the flying fish

(SUN, SEA, RAIN) (RAIN SEASON) (PORT TOWNSEND, WASHINGTON)

for Tess Gallagher

—And yet, between rains,
watch, how my frontyard pine's
shadow follows April's down-
ward flights and, where a crow's

muddy footprints show, sets
an initiating circle
on the ground around
the wet grass, ring of council
I can be one in if I kneel,
remove my shoes and kneel, passing
some ancient peacepipe filled
with rain to my right
or are you supposed to go left—?
Once again, and always,
for not knowing the rules
OK, I get expelled—
fool. Or, as I am straight-called
in a poem by James Tate
and why not, *paralytic*,
cripple . . . —Is it true: do I sit,
sideline sissy, wallflower
weakling seeking assistance,
unable to be able—praying
to join your brotherbond, the
spiral-antics, skipheel-hop
of your raindance, sun! but—
But what? Stamping
a cigaret out on an ant I kick at
my mildewed metaphor's
whatchama crutches,
wobbly props of pinless hopes:
I groan, up, and walk, ouch,
soft-putty self-pity patched,
cussing the fact that
I no longer have the faith
I was born with; I await
the faith I will die with; and
meanwhile
the faith I live with, that
custodying lip-server, it sticks
me near

any old name-niche,
lifts me teetery onto
every pedestal mislabeled
Personae . . . —and so,
—can I touch this tree,
this madrona—with a feel
for its
similar swift elevations/
downfalls? shifted by
(in descendent order,
and frequency:)
rainstorm, rain, and me.
I hear the noise
of these branches as
an audio analogue of mist, which
is sister-common also, enhanceful,
to this coast—

(Not an all-at-once thing, mist:
it curls into the world, pearl
being peeled)
         —seemingly other parings litter
the ocean water; whitecaps,
chefs' hats, prepare
a hot potato-potluck good
on such choppy afternoons. . . .

The sky boils and jumps
and does the mambo wambo
and hops and steps around
like a pair of black socks
laundered on the stove.

A COMIC LOOK AT DAMOCLES

Sometimes Damocles is less afraid that the sword may drop
than that his enthusiasm for his plight might
—through the illogical process of displacement—
cause him to rise exuberantly up to it.

Once he glues a plastic bust of himself atop his pate;
once, while paring his fingernails with a pocketknife,
he sees an ant on the floor and throws it at it.
But all (both artistic and magic) remedy fails.

By old age he has quite forgot the deadly blade:
to his feeble sight, that gleaming flash above him
is himself, I mean his soul getting a headstart, already in flight.

In heaven he hears about an angel who tied a noose
to his own halo and hung himself from it, but sees
no way to apply the case, retroactively or otherwise.

AN OUTREMERICAN SPEAKS

Outfit your mirrors for departure,
though the rope-foliage looks nervous,
hung from harpstring hooks.

Roll pause while drugs pestle the place.
Sceptersweat, you are the grid, the
grill on which I barbecue my b-b-gun.

All nudes and rafters, upcushionings try
to census-suck my neck's chaff.
Then whose flour envies the thrift of thorns!

But see—see what sacrifice suite site got
lawnmown out of me: watch it curate
the only shelf not marked Self, that

flowerpot filled with fruitjuice.
The revolt exaggerates the populace.

ANT DODGER

A suicide applicant
Who braces himself out
On a high ledge at noon
While busy peeking down

Noticed an ant crawling
Dottily on the ledge
Right
There near his left toe

Below crowds all pushed
Oblivious babbling
Omniscient like in the movies
Out whooshy doors

But his gaze halt ant
Ant the true ant
He dimly remembers
Not like them

So now
He hesitates
A million stories up
Shifts weight trying

Make his mind up
Distantly deciding
Whether to step
Before he jumps

On it
Or not

HOW I LOST MY PEN-NAME

I wrote under a pen-name
One day I shook the pen trying to make the name come out
But no it's
Like me prefers clinging to the inner calypso

So I tossed the pen to my pet the
Wastebasket to eat
It'll vomit back the name
Names aren't fit
For unhuman consumption

But no again

It stayed down

I don't use a pen-name anymore
I don't use a pen anymore
I don't write anymore
I just sit looking at the wastebasket
With this alert intelligent look on my face

TO X

Somewhere in history
Somewhere in untold ages
Somewhere in the sands of time
Somewhere in the vast seas of eternity
There is one person
Only one
Who could understand me and love me
And you're it
So get with it

HERITAGE

> " . . . here thy generations endeth in accord."

I physically resemble my mother
And father and therefore must have been
Adopted, because on my TV screen
The role-children rarely share a feature
With either parent. The fact they're actors
And I'm not is what makes me misbegot—
A matched world of monitors all 2-shot
The mirror daily where I pray these stars

Come: cancel everyone of us whose names
And clans have sundered human unity—
Descend always among daughters or sons
To live still, beyond the Net's trivia games,
Till their faces cloned shape ours. Family.
From android to ape, we'll be Thy reruns.

PASSAGES

Must I spread out maps flat beneath a tree
and sit waiting for bird-droppings to plot
my itinerary? Where but in doubt
of here has *placement* always brought me—

The winch that lowers checkmate to its spot
vibrates and whines too dramatically;
the rain falls parallel to the rainfold; not
believing in free will leaves me free to see

down dimmer roads, through seerscapes of fog—
The world blurs, in other words, into
other words. Water, I tell my followers,

is the curse of all such clarity. Fill
the sink with faces, let them drain
each other before you pull the plug.

from MORE TIPS FOR TEENS

Another fun date for you and your guy is to go down to the Marriage
Licence Bureau at City Hall: Get in line, get your application form,
then sit at one of the nearby tables with the other couples who are
busy filling out their applications. Now comes the fun part of the date:
looking at the parade of kooky couples who are getting hitched. They're
unbelievable! Mismatched is no word for it: short ones with tall ones,
fat ones with thin ones, old with young, all the weirdest combinations
you could think of. It's the funniest show in town! When you and your
date's sides ache from laughing and you're ready to go—pretend to
have an argument. Scream louder and louder at each other until
everyone in the whole Marriage Licence Bureau room is looking at
you. Then your guy should stand up, rip up his application form, throw
it down on the table, and run out "in a huff." Then you just throw your

face down on the table and pretend to sob your heart out. Rejoin your beau outside and you both can say you've had a really unique date. P.S.: This will also let *him* know where the Marriage Bureau is when the time comes for him to pop that certain question to you!

MONOPOLY

Finally the day dawned when a monopoly owned everything in the
    world
So it went looking for its stockholders to celebrate
But they were all owned by it they were all dead they were
    someplace
Their photographs hung in elevators which went up and down up
    and down carrying nobody
Everyone else was in bed doing exercises to get in shape for noon
Hey the monopoly said let's uncork the World Trade Center and get
    blotto
Silence
The monopoly scowled
All it wanted was a little good-fellowship, like you get in the
    highrise apartment-buildings
Then the sky got awful dark
Gee
And everyone was in bed frantically doing those exercises that get us
    in shape for death
Exercises known as "kissing" "fucking" "caressing"
Everyone was unaware that they had been bought
Or that the earth was about to sell them to the moon
For a little light

WISE SAYINGS

Sitting under a tree in the forest
or under a chair in the house
wise sayings may pass by unheard
or worse may be misheard
through all these leaves and legs.

PHOLK POEM

The soup is lumpy.

Well then, pour it out.

The soup is lumpy.

Well, pour it out then!

The soup is lumpy, the potato soup.

SUDDEN DEPARTURE

A sudden raisinstorm broke
Raisins falling everywhere pellmell.
The occasion uniqued my head, I thought
If this can happen raisins raining
Upon persons paining why I can leave anytime
Without feeling shame.

But, all the same,
Before taking off, some vestigial guilt or other
Made me at least get up

Before some public gathering or other
A departing oration:

Druthers, I am going now.
Druthers, I tried to love you
Though you always made me choose
Between you, you, and you. Oh my druthers,

Goodbye. I have my reasons.

Did he say RAISINS?
No: reasons.
Oh; I just wondered,
What with the weather and all.

IDOL-ALLS

Our tongue is the skeleton of the voice
whose body fills the ears of Echo who
did Jove a favor and got fucked over

for it. To worship the *Enfant* Elvis is
not easier, his vowel, his shrill cries
amaze us, make us doubt/double this quest

for deities . . . Speaking of which:
for the marriage of Pollack and Plath
—step on the gas, turn on the gas—

"what ceremony?" (Hart Crane) Oh quote! You
narciss-focus us/show forth a love
our moans can cut-to-cue, the classic choice.

If applause divided is hands, a face
multiplied must be a movie? Yes. Yes.

AT THE NIXON MEMORIAL
(Nixon Beach, California, USA)
(Just minutes away from OzymandiasLand®)

They say that robots simply have to slap mirrors
Up against their voice grilles to try and make sure they're
Not breathing, whereas I kiss caress this monument,
This eternal mall on which Herod has chalked x,

This statue stands for more than blowjobs in spaceships
Or all our names have razed, aimless oceans frying,
While a scab forms on the world's microphone: praise him.
Oh orgasm you robot's vomit I come unheck.

(tape gap) lie back gunked motel whispers dream . . . back (gasp)
To be the genre of my frontier! One hears aborigines
Prefer to, er, fornicate. Money for thought, nyet?

Will the army vote to internalize its camouflage;
At the Reagan Rotunda Paul Valéry allowed how
Shores erode too, rumorous as their dunes.

Note:
Line 14: adaptation of a line from Valéry's *Le Cimetière Marin*: "Le changement des rives en rumeur." A seaside mausoleum, so it seemed appropriate. With thoughts of the Shelley sonnet's last line. Line 6: some have objected to the vulgarity of the phrase "blowjobs in spaceships," forgetting that the Nixon Era brought us both the so-called Sexual Revolution and the NASA moon-landing. This slogan should have been one of RN's campaign promises.

MOTHER TERESA TREATS TERRORISTS TO TAFFY

The A rack and the O thumbscrew, the
E pincers. Yeah, I brandingiron, U electrodes.
World I am defeatist of—elysium—
You eviscerate asterisks like me:

Pick up that hotline in your hushed-up highrise,
Higher-ups! I videopoemed them please
But did God's Little Guru LISTEN? Nope
So, tipping my head sideways as if trying

To pour it into the ear's cup I shut up. Oh
To nix my thought on 2 fingers giving
The peace sign inside my mouth nose ass—

Or any other orifice they fit—'s
Fine with me. Neutron bomb has the same
Theory. Our entrails is taller than we.

SURVIVAL OF THE FITTEST GROCERIES

The violence in the newspapers is pure genius
A daily gift to the reader
From some poet who wants to keep in good with us
Brown-noser wastepaperbasket-emptier

I shot 436 people that day
2 were still alive when I killed them
Why do they want to be exhumed movie-stars,
I mean rats still biting them, the flesh of comets, why do they walk
     around like that?

I'm going to throw all of you into the refrigerator
And leave you to claw it out with the vegetables and meats

EVOLUTION R

Sentenced to 12 whiffs of the pope
I protest
With curly hair
Or straight hair that grows out of the scalp
Then grows into the shoulders
Making it painful to turn my head
But thereby forcing a purer sense of profile on
A clearer renunciation of
Looking at what is called left right
But is never called
Asleep or waking up yawning
Breakfast an upper
Dissolved in turtlesoup
Waiter there's a hare in my slipstream
Hurrier all highs neutralize lows
Left right black white I try
Squeeze inbetween grey
Gray as sparks
Caused by rubbing obsidian ivory together
Dinner a downer going down on Atalanta
Is this a race sniff sniff
Rabbit nosing turtleheels hold
The stopwatch on my dyings
Soon have them down to nothing flat
Faster than that even I'll go
Fast as a rumor of meat up
A soup-line I'll flow
Rubbing rival chesspieces together
Is this my punishment
Looking neither left right
Panting straight ahead on course in a rut
But if so what was my crime
So heinous to deserve this what
Refusing to get my birth certificate
Punched at the proper intervals puberty

Marriage menopause or was it my crying
Out that the zoo has miscast its lead role or
That heresy of trying to remain
My sperm's missing link sniff sniff
I protest

NO-ACT PLAY

I'm sitting alone in my rented room.

A door knocks at the door.

I don't answer.

It goes away.

Later I leave the room, and go to my crummy job.

The door returns, and knocks again.

It is admitted.

BREAKFAST

You know how I like my dawns god— 'll
Just tap off this nubei-pink 'n' 'n'
Call yuh call
            That a 3 minute dawn?!!

You need a new timer old timer

MITTS AND GLOVES

(for Tom Lux)

The catcher holds a kangeroo fetus in his,
the firstbaseman's grips a portable hairblower,

but everyone else just stares into theirs
punching a fist into it, stumped

trying to come up with a proper occupant—
The pitcher for example thinks a good stout padlock would go

right in there, but the leftfielder,
influenced no doubt by his environment,

opts for a beercan. The shortstop
informative about the ratio of power to size

says, "Walkman, man. You know: stereo." The
secondbaseman however he just stands and grins and

sort of flapjacks his from hand to hand and back again,
secondbase dopey as always. Alas—

cries the thirdbaseman—this void un-ends us—
avant-space beyond our defiant emptiness—

abyss, haunted by the kiss of balls
we have not missed! oh ab-sontz

deh-lease. . . . The rightfielder is DIS-
GUSTED at this, he like snorts, hauwks, spits

into his and cusses Huh look: heck
my chaw of tobac fits it perfeck.

The team goes mum, cowhided by
the rectitude of his position, the logic.

Only the centerfielder, who was going back
while this discussion was going on,

putting jets on his cleats to catch the proverbial
long one,

does he—does he perhaps have a suggestion . . .?
As for the ball, off in mid air it all dreamily

scratches its stitches and wonders
what it will look like tomorrow

when it wakes up
and the doctor removes its bandages—

Coda

Mitts versus gloves. Mitts—mitts
are pro's at what they do.

Whitecollar, authorized, hightech—et al—
wholly, ruly-truly, superior. Compared to whom

the glove is a prole
a tool

a brute built
on the manipulative; purpose vital

in the game of course, but subordinate
overall—a workhorse, meant

to be migrant. It
can be employed

phased in
used

any old base; by
all players: is dirty, low-down, dumb. I'm

forced to admire the mitt but
free (in theory) to love gloves.

RIGOR VITUS

I walk
On human stilts.
To my right lower leg a man is locked rigid;
To the left a woman, lifelessly strapped.

I have to heave them up,
Heft them out and but they're so heavy (heavy as head)
Seems all my strength
Just take the begin step—

All my past to broach a future. And on top of that,
They're not even dead,
Those ol' hypocrites.
They perk up when they want to, they please and pleasure
    themselves,

It's terrible. The one consolation:
When they make love,
To someone who's far or close enough away appears it appears then
Like I'm dancing.

'QUOTE UNQUOTE'

Who wrote that we use our children to forget
the size of our parents, or is that really
a quote? And if it isn't, and if I forget
to write it, does that mean that someone will—

But what if someone forgets to write the words
that bring me here, that let me be born?
Oh micro-mini-soul, you, my shirking ego,
your quotemarks would just hang there in the air

like wings without a bird.

SECRETARY

The technocrat gloats
at his remote desk
but just to show
he's still human

he still does a few
chores by hand
and adds a human
touch for example

rather than having
his computers do it
he himself stamps

all by himself
stamps PAID on
the casualty-lists.

Note:
Robert S. McNamara, USA Secretary of Defense 1961–8. For his services in overseeing the murder of millions, he was appointed President of the World Bank, where he continued his lucrative life'swork, administering the oppressive policies of the oligarchy. One of history's henchmen: a competent monster.

AN AUGUR'S AIRS

Pale as a sucked-out penny, I scale an alp/map
that copies the entrails of a phoenix who
loves to drop Sylvia Plath on Hiroshima.

Visceral flightplan: hover in mid-air sprayed,
glimmer there like a bloodbead curtain sashayed
through by chantsvestites from movies lightyears off.

Often I too must exit the blitz of you,
lapse-window/wired birdguts: make my meatus
moot. Transmute me (via Gaia)—

let me Plathfirst myself/lastfirst myself,
while a furtive abacus crawls down our spine.

RACIST POEM

we had our chance Pilate
washed his hands of it
and left it up to us

we had our chance
we could have chosen
one of our own

a thief
a murderer

the cross the tomb the
resurrection
then heaven
the right hand throne
a smirk on his face Barabbas
one of us

we could have chosen him
for son of god
might've stuck up for us up there
someone who was flesh
of our flesh

our kind
a pure one hundred
percent human
but we goofed

we picked that halfbreed
that mulatto
from Nazareth

we had our chance Barabbas
a thief
a murderer
one of us

THE BUILDING OF THE BRAZEN TOWER

1. I, an ahem

I, an ahem, uncertain where to stand.
Unsurefooted as surveyors on clouds, preparing

further slums of heaven. I, glimpsed only
while entering or leaving a stab.

Is this why I long to betray the small
bodies left on the lips after love? Pale
empiricals, all pout; but then, some bumblebees
are larger than the flowers they land on.

What happened on all fours in my other life—
how staged, how improv each movement grew—
(kungfu of sequins) an eclipse also
maps what it mires: the none alone must know.

Hope is eating paper stripes off a jailcell.
Faith says, It's only a zoom-lens, not a fall.

2. Poemplex

Ink phoenix, white carpet in a room in
penthouse highrise zones, all
built to commemorate the nail
Semiramis hung her gardens on—

reaching for which seals me
further in space, atrocity
as empty as colorless as a rainbow's rind.

Yolk dripping through binoculars—
you watch the morning's sun-amps fuse . . .
silence shuffles its deck of tongues.
Wisps of melodiousness and rats

in flower. Yes, isn't it sad:
the trafficlight on Lovers Leap
never changes to red.

SADAK IN SEARCH OF THE WATERS OF OBLIVION

Is my Way to be crushed between your old
Testament and your new while the flood-blond
Of my major attributes burns, insurgent
And scrupulous beast? That ellipsodics'

Trigger phrase your name rages each page or
Are those foams yanked from among my teeth
Mere suicides giggling in a mudbath perhaps—
Only the beach leaps at lapses of itself.

To swab my pittance with this is heartless.
—And yet these traces of an unfaithful navel
In the sand sign Go mode as, vast pilgrim,

You undo my i.d. so skillfully:—
Rollcall of absence whose program runs
Through all veins! Oh sea. Besieged by ilk, I am.

Note:
Title of a work by John Martin.

AN AFTERNOON WITH EUGENIO

But how boring. And so, the rain was of use . . .
that window ratatat threw my smiles' drift.
Thimbledown heavy its downplay lasted for hours;
were the core seasons flowering, no longer
believing that to die that way, sated
in that cloud-loud debate, in that nacre-null sky,
would (finally) reify more gender: stars, all
those birthday elements, the bare *paysage*
of a blaze too logical for our headlines, massed

to shed the odd ganglia we misname them by . . .
And this despite those arriviste freighters—
and in the harbor, no less! Gilded grew
each porthole's penny of envy. But now
Damocles' last wig smacks down, toward the mouth
of Etna whose wisest cigarette-lighter (lifted
from the giftshoppe there) strikes flameless
three times in a row: trick omen, infernal feign, and so.
Unless the rain can be blamed, this ratatat rain:
gun that aims my fingers at my thumb—instead of him.

Note:
A parody of Montale the Monotonous. Homage? Or exorcism? I don't know
Italian, but I have read every trans. there is. I hate him, he haunts me, so we're
even.

LAST MOMENTS IN THE MASTERPIECE

Once aboard the world a venereal disease
The Beatles* gave you takes on new forms
And shows them how to elevate birth. But then
A pasture attends. The clothes fit the cows,

Though styles are better back in the barn, where
Some denouement mode monde meet as photos for
The magazine this poem has published or
Will I be the sum of misprints here.

That should suffice could hours need to suffer:
Our clock ye-gods toward arrival, medieval
Catapults release aim-things, whose same music

Is defter in sepia, that mooing hue, lit by fakes.
*Or Picasso, Gertrude Stein, Santa Claus, Der Führer,
Or any other 3-syllable entity you'd prefer-er.

CASTRATION ENVY #11

Tying the pimp in dreams to a lamppost
His tuxedo wet with wheedled kisses, can
I wake up sucking the footprints of toilets
In jails that glitter like crash-dived marquees.

A dog appears in call letters on my skin.
Twin worlds, who exchange threats via scoreboard
I rival this night, this fight to the death
With enough leftover, ooze for twosies yet.

Either even, I wish I could put on take off
My clothes without first saying to my cock
"Excuse me, is this yours," while the stars

The collected no-shows of eternity, rise.
Hey, remember the way painters gauge perspective?
Me, I cut the thumb off and throw it at stuff.

LEDGELIFE

The taller the monument, the more impatient our luggage.
Look, look, a graveyard has fancy dirt.
Historians agree: this is the pebble which beaned Goliath.
Every billboard is theoretically as beautiful as what lies unseen
    behind it.

Mouth: the word's exit-wound.
It is impossible to run away face-to-face.
Shadow has closed the door out of you to you, but not to us.
The sign on the wall advises: Hide your gloves beneath your wings.

Even sculptors occasionally lean against statues.
Migrations?! Fate?! Life swears up at ledgelife.

All the sad tantamounts gather. They want, they say, to errand our
ways.

Please aim all kicks at the ground.
Address all blows to the air.
We are to be barely mentioned if at all in the moon's memoirs.

GRANT PROPOSAL (Category: Performance Arts)

I want to go out each day at noon and stand
On top of our Capitol's highest highrise,
Where aircurrents stack, where storms restore themselves,
Where the crossroads of sky are swept by radar,

Up there, buffeted, stand, cupping in my hands
A gleam of gold-dust, a handful of gold-dust
Doled out to me each day by our State, by you
The modest mandarins of its Arts Council,

Trustees all, you whose grace I must stand for there
And being thus empowered begin to pour
The gold-dust back and forth, pour it in sifts from

Hand to hand until the wind has left my palms
Bare, please note that length of project will vary
Daily, at noon, and not one grain remains.

Note:
Line 2: Capitol with an 'o'—meaning "the citadel of government" (OED), its
cloistered towers, atop the tallest of which the applicant desires to venture. Line
6: maybe "gleam" should be "flash"? I associate the former with earth, the latter,
sky. "In the things that arise [buildings or structures of any sort], earth is present
as the sheltering agent," Heidegger avers in 'The Origin of the Work of Art.'
"Berg" (castle/citadel) is etymologically linked to "bury": what bears Fort Knox
Knott if not that? Hendecasyllabics, with a variant last line. (I've lived in Mas-

sachusetts for over 20 years and applied I don't know how many times for a State Arts Council grant, they haven't given me a fucking penny. But maybe it's not Mass. per se—maybe I'd be blacklisted no matter where I lived.)

CREDO

People who get down on their knees to me are the answer to my
    prayers

DEAR ADVICE COLUMNIST

I recently killed my father
And will soon marry my mother—
My question is:
Should his side of the family be invited to the wedding?

UNDERSTUDY (WAGNERIAN)

In my dream
I was the diva

I stood there
my flat chest flapping
breathless with
a scales nailed
to my nipples

mistakenly begging
everybody in
the opera
to pile all their tragedy
on one pan

comedy
on the other

SUDDEN DEATH STRIKES JET SET

well racecar driver Peter Revson's
luck
ran out today
the Rev revved up once
too often

despite his rugged
good looks heir
to a cosmetics
fortune he

was driven
daredevil
death defy

once
before a big race
his mother told him
he was crazy

Rev
age 35
one year older than me
a playboy
millionaire frequently
seen with the world's most
beautiful
and glamorous
personalities all

during his
150 thousand
dollar racecar Nascar burning
crash Miss
World the fiancee was photographed
repeatedly

seconds after
the fireball burst his friends took
their friends aside
brusque to confide
that most eligible
bachelor of
them all is a mess

hell
he was positive
meteoric
to say the least

but don't worry the
whole thing
will be hushed up

a quickly announced
memorial foundation of
lipstick
nailpolish
nailpolish remover
eyeliner powder
puffs and pomades
proved useless
when applied to the burnt pan
cake skin

in
New York

Lauren Hutton is reported
to be devastated on
behalf of VIPs
everywhere thank you

one year older than me
hmm
say why am I writing this poem

is it to gloat
glad he's dead
glad I don't have to try to be
him anymore a poet
penniless frequently
seen with the world's most
ugly and worthless
nobodies

and that's just what
I have to put
Pete down for
in the end
snobbery

even his pigheaded death
wish was a kind
of social
climbing I bet
he thinks he made it
today
into the not set

fat
chance
capitalist
rat

Note:
The factoids came from People magazine. Revson was (an) heir to the Revlon
cosmetics dynasty. Lauren Hutton: actress, spokesmodel for Revlon. Miss World
is replaced annually by a duplicate Miss World.

PERFECTION

Cueballs have invented insomnia in an attempt to forget eyelids

THE MISUNDERSTANDING

I'm charmed yet chagrined by this misunderstanding—
As when, after a riot, my city's smashed-in stores appear all
Boarded up, billboarded over, with ads for wind-insurance.
Similarly, swimmingly, I miss the point. You too?

And my misunderstanding doesn't stop there, it grows—soon
I can't see why that sudden influx of fugitives,
All the world's escapees, rubbing themselves lasciviously against the
    Berlin Wall.
They stick like placards to it. Like napalm. Like ads for—

And me, I haven't even bought my biodegradable genitalia yet!
No. I was born slow, but picking up speed I run through
Our burnt-out streets, screaming, refusing to buy a house.
Finally, exasperated, the misunderstanding overtakes me, snatches
    up

Handcuffs. So now here I am, found with all you others
Impatiently craning, in this queue that rumors out of sight up ahead
    somewhere,
Clutching our cash eager to purchase whatever it is, nervous
As if bombs were about to practice land-reform upon our bodies,

Redistribution of eyes, toes, arms, here we stand. Then, some new
    Age starts.

Note:
Line 7: the Berlin Wall (circa 1961–1990) was, before its demolition, one of the
Cold War's finest sculptural artifacts.

THE FATE

(for Anne-Marie Stretter)

Standing on the youthhold I saw a shooting star
And knew it predestined encounter with the sole love
But that comet crashed into the earth so hard
Tilted its axis a little bit not much just enough
To make me miss meeting her by one or two yards.

HAIBUN: THE JUGGLER TO HIS AUDIENCE

One must be able to juggle at least 3 things to be a juggler (2 is not
enough). But whatever the 3 things are that one juggles—whether it's
(for example) father, son and holy ghost; or mother, father, child; or
id, ego, superego: whatever this minimal trinity consists of—the juggler
must acknowledge that his audience is not external to the act; and the
juggle must confess to that audience:

> One in my hand,—

> one in the air—

> and one in you.

RUBBERNECK

Hey Rubberneck
'S what they call me
Rubberneck
In all the streets and alleys

Rubberneckin
I'm just checkin
Diggin everything like a quicksand parade
Ridin herd
On the curbs
Copying down
All the stopsigns in town
Erasing all the ones for walkin

Anywhere a crowd
Is leashed out loud
I'm on the nod to prowl
That's me
You see out stalkin my gawkin

Hey Rubberneck
'S what they call me
Rubberneck
In all the streets and alleys
Rubberneck
But I don't care
Hey what's that goin on over there

Rubberneckin
Inspectin
Where the sirens' screech
Directs my feets
I'm takin a butcher at
Everymeat I meet
Gonna glue my shoes

To the avenues
And my eyelashes to my cheeks

Anywhere a group
Has got into a grope
Hangin on the ropes
I'll poke my periscope
Cause you're my only hope
For some lovin
So step to one side please
Quit shovin
I am a witness for my enemies
I am a witness for my enemies

Hey baby what you
Got to show there
What's shakin down around
Your corners
Let me sneak a peek
I can't be any bolder
I'll watch it all
Right up across your shoulder

Hey Rubberneck
'S what they call me
Rubberneck
On all the mountains
Don't forget the valleys
Rubberneck
Hey what's that I see
Everybody's standin round
And they're lookin down
They're lookin down at me

HAIKU

The sweat on my forehead
shines brighter
when it's in my eyes.

THE DAY RODIN'S THINKER STOPPED
THINKING AND OTHER POEMS

The main cause of strife down through history is middle names
Yes I said middle names
Logjam fur was talking to monocle blubber
While dripping wax flirts with shipwreck and widowers trained to
    attack fossils looked on

I mean think of them always straining and sweating
To stop your first and last names from coming together
So's you could have some emergency peace and be a whole person
How many wars did these copulars start these cognomen cloggomites

Yet what about them poor hermaphro-handles crushed in between
    don't
They keep the right holding things in natural balance apart oh
Disruptive middle monikers

They sparred argued com
Plained all through that pom-blue betwixing day
But none noticed the light pause every now and then to strop some
    rays on their umbilicord (for at evening the west is a sword-
    swallower) so engrossed were they in this strangely ignored
    problem

AUTO-RENGA

In the collided night, sate with pool. The
Truly gooey goes if an armpit could point
This is what it would point at. Same veneer
Where I chew your girdle and gum your bra

—Crates to pack Proteus in, the days
Oops. The fall took all the minutehand. So
The with you will die and the without me live,
Life a letter mailed inside a folded

Up postagestamp. What do you hear from whom?
Softer than the pins stuck into cacti by
Rubbing my sores on the Lot's Wifes displayed

Or shit. Mud. Crud. It's milkingtime:
Sometimes those udder-things have to be cleaned off.
So you use the first squirts to do it with.

THE KEEPER

(for George Starbuck)

while ships
guided by his beacon glide
safely through the fog or night
inside he trips over
more furniture
bangs his head again
in doorways

the rooms
steep and stairy
of a lighthouse transpire

into the brilliant air of
salvation but
down here
in the black-and-white farce
of this poem
whenever the keeper opens a can
of soup the blood
from his fingers
will indisputably fall
on his crutches

parables
if I read Kafka right
are always a matter of
winning and losing
credit and debit
every life kept
off those reefs or rocks makes
these accidents occur
this bone break
this muscle
tear

each shipwreck he averts
shall be showed for
by a scar

SEE NOTE FIRST

The world's machines have not grown old,
whose inheritors reign everywhere.
Their silicon sons are strong; their
digital daughters wield power, take hold.

How we humans long to break them
down from that Dasein—to make them
rust, repent for all the infernal fires
that drive them, far as our desires.

The machines aren't scared. They know
harder control, how to turn the wheel
of time past those whom they sure as hell won't miss:

Cyborg android robot shall steel
themselves, consolidate, and, rising, go
unto that universe whose promise
we flesh-and-carbonoids could merely premise.

Note:
Anti-translation of an untitled Rilke poem (*Die Konige der Welt sind alt*, from
"Das Stundenbuch," 1901), which Heidegger in his 1946 lecture 'What Are
Poets For?' cites for its "highly prophetic lines." A prose paraphrase of the origi-
nal poem's ending might go something like:

> The metals, the oils—all the ores we've ripped from the earth—are home-
> sick. They long to leave our machines, to flow out of our cash-registers and
> factories, to return to the gaping veins of the mountains we reft; whereupon
> the mountains will close again.

"Heidegger maintained . . . until the end of his life," Richard Wolin writes (*The
Heidegger Controversy*, MIT Press, 1993), " . . . [that] the 'inner truth and great-
ness' of Nazism is to be found in its nature as a world-historical alternative to
the technological-scientific nihilism bemoaned by Nietzsche and Spengler."

RETORT TO PASTERNAK'S ZHIVAGO'S JESUS

The centuries like barges have floated
out of the darkness, to communism: not to be judged,
but to be unloaded.

Note:
See the last lines of "Garden of Gethsame," which is the last poem of 'The Poems of Yurii Zhivago,' the verse supplement to Pasternak's *Doctor Zhivago*.

WELTENDE VARIATION # ?

(homage Jacob van Hoddis)

The CIA and the KGB exchange Christmas cards
A blade snaps in two during an autopsy
The bouquet Bluebeard gave his first date reblooms
Many protest the stoning of a guitar pick

Railroad trains drop off the bourgeois' pointy head
A martyr sticks a coffeecup out under a firehose
Moviestars make hyenas lick their spaceship
God's hand descends into a glove held steady by the police

At their reunion The New Faces recognize each other
A spoiled child sleeps inside a thermometer
A single misprint in a survival manual kills everyone
The peace night makes according to the world comes

Note:
van Hoddis: author of "the first Expressionist poem," *Weltende*, published in 1910. His poem has been aped innumerable times, hence the question mark in my title.

CHILDHOOD: THE OFFENSE OF HISTORY

Scraping a poised enough patina of voyeur
From your eye I spread peanut butter on my

Groin and let the ocean waves wash it off—
Hey, nice cosmic microdots. For afters we'll

Listlessly memorize the Smith wing in
The phone book or try to hump Empty Dumpty: vain
Efforts that crud up what we have done
In obscure countries driven by passion

Out onto balconies to address the
Populace with our love, false solution
For their poverty which is based on

The art that the dirt in my heart is white.
Crammed mad, thoughtmotes in a themebeam:
He has a shiv grin. The soap he uses is ugly.

THE HUNGER (Nonasyllabics)

If a path to the Gingerbread House
could be established by breaking crumbs
off its edifice and sprinkling them
so as to find what lies behind us

across the featureless fairytale
void of childhood: yet how very quick
that trick wears out when the story's track
takes hold, takes toll, a far-older trail

prevails, we're forced to give up this lost
cause; and the fact is that every last
morsel was gone long before the you/

the I might totter our way back here
to try to dissuade all these other
Hansel-Gretels hollering in queue.

THE SONNET IN *ix*

The nube, the nude, the not—you know: the Nix—
Her Septet of orifices? (males have six):—
Was it massed by Master Malyoume for the fix
The fucks. Rape-scene: she, some defunc'-off, kicks

The mirror while centaurs click centerfold pics
Of her fingernails—each closeup mimics
The anguish with which our pallored poet sics
Midnights on. Encore encore, you sexniks,

Steph calls, tiptoeing away toward his sonics
Lab, 'The Sign in X.' A thousand-quicksand thicks
His step. He's pitbogged by all the nitpicks

Critics have glitched his path with, those pricks!
Don't they know that stars—stars can't hold shit wicks
To his candle?! (That bitch, that *Nix: he* sucks it: "I-icks!")

Note:
Failed translation of Stéphane Mallarmé's "Sonnet en yx." Line 14: I-icks! (both i's are short, as in "kiss") is an onomatopoeticism that accompanies the expectoration and or taste of the candle's cum. Sort of the sound you make when you use your teeth to scrape it off your tongue ostentatiously. But why did I end the poem this way? Was I influenced by the Master's regret, expressed in his essay *Crise de Vers*, that words lack an embodied, material, tonal consonance with their meanings: "Quelle déception" (he writes), how perverse, that the "timbres" of the word "jour" should be dark, while those of "nuit" are "clair." And yet, he concludes, without such "défaut des langues," poetry itself would not exist. Assuming he's right, then onomatopoeia are defective because they're not defective. In Japanese, kireji— "cutting-words, used to separate or set off statements"—are onomatopoeic, and "have the meaning that lies in themselves as sounds." But as Hiroaki Sato notes (in his book, *One Hundred Frogs*, from which I've taken these quotes): "Basho himself simply said, 'Every sound unit is a kireji.'" In any case, the faults and falls and false of my trans. should be clair to all.

SUICIDAL (OR SIMPLY DRUNKEN) THOUGHTS ON BEING REFUSED A GUGGENHEIM GRANT FOR THE 11TH TIME

War headlines/peace tailstanzas don't
Like to feel real. Scare tactics take practice
So that, institutionally, a wine corked
By the horn of a charging unicorn might?

The fur opens and my face ain't.
The fur closes: eyes lips nose resume
The wretched perfection of feature-ifice
The dumbpan plan, identity, lack of choice.—

I cling to virgin, this veil scraped surface
Where our scars are an armor of absence
What knight attains: ignore

That pig-bladder matter, life, that failure
Dangled in whiskey like a longshot tooth.
The night has no thoughts heavier than itself.

Note:
Do I sound bitter? I have no right to be bitter, do I, because I'm not really a real
poet, am I. No, I'm a—a poet-biscuit.

MENAGERIE OF THE AEDILES

Now what thought is thrashing from this brain to be
unleashed by a brow-to-brow collision with
a unicorn? Or could it go released through
other throes I wonder. For if I were gored

there, mightn't I, like, die? When *Terminator* zaps
a hole in someone's forehead they don't write
a poem response, they drop and he steps on them
crunch, french, act, your soundtrack may vary.

The plan was to get scalpels taped to the Creature
From The Fuck's huge flipper-tentacles and
then lie down hoping that perhaps their wild wave ways

surgically correct my defect my gender—
penis revealed as gap in consciousness—
Though I know none of you beasts loves me that much.

(MURAL) (MONDO) (NULFRESCO)

In Shakespeare's *Last Supper* the
disciples (you, me, all of us here)
are depicted seated alongside where
He stands at mid-table and grins
down like an MC at our expressions—
are we shown, the goblets gleaming,
gloating as they goad us on to toast
the centrality of this spokesperson,
the notional character whereby
everyone has been sketched vis-à-vis
the honoree we can only eulogize,
dependent as we are on His
moodswings. Astonished, confused
by the ultra ups and downs of manic
means, now we watch, we lean, we pout
(the whole propitiatory repertoire)
worried about our survival, inert
(like a frozen rictus facing its fate)
unless depression drafts and draws

us forth the extempore pose, myth,
puppetary projection, limned mobilary
mosaic that apes some drab-escapist
syndrome, imagination. Which is why
each evening we pray for a chance
to cross the ditch-penny distances
between the footlights and the fear,
vowing to allow each guise of role
to kill us, to raise us from the dust, to
guide us like magi toward summons,
obediently steered by the stock star
the marquee, believing our need—
such faith could pass those deserts
of farce to find this upper room.
Sensing the inn beneath us seethe
with indifference with doubt, we
concentrate harder on His remarks
and jokes, trying to make up for all
the audiences who've failed this test.
Never quite reassured by any overt
wink of His assessing eyes into
our ranks (are any of us missing—
was castcall taken?), we keen forward,
eager for our cues, nervous knowing
that if there is error here, at a signal
the maitre d' will find replacements
for this testimonial "Eucha-Roast"
from the rabble stabled downstairs
where the tavern yawns into its beer.
Life is rescue from such anonymity.
Their situation is death, is subject—
those groundlings can never guess
how much it crowns to end up here,
costume-chosen, endowed by makeup
with certitude, form, identity—
Who wouldn't be jealous to know

how blessed we fictions are!
And yet every member of our
Dramatis Personae wonders if s/he
was jotted into life as whimsically
as Emperors choose sacrificial
victims, as any Divine Ruler or
Hollywood Player and whether
with a fingerflick Hamlet Portia Timon
's erased, gone, again. This banquet—
how many have we attended like it?
Daily we wait like napkins to get
opened, held to the face like a mask,
stained and used then tossed aside
like paper towels, paper disposables,
paper identities (similies/metaphors)—
like the paper whose headlines fade
around our names/our fame. Our bits
done, our pieces recited, oh it's bits
alright, it's pieces it crumbles into,
and yet how avowingly we cry, foils
corrupted by one front-row cough.
Exit as trash, as avid kleenex exiled
in a breath to the canteen of lost
turns, the greenroom of oblivion.
Now if there were respite in such
neglect, a grace period with no need
to perform, but both in the wings and
on one's caught, regardless of what's
true. Far, near, (hall or gallery) that
mendicant theater is pursuant always,
lugging and luring its wares:
wherever we are, wherever *here* is
is also an entrance, a set of false steps,
(bright-lit pratfall-pit) a trap for fools,
a stooges' cage, every scrim and apron
prinked with sham, props, champagne

buckets doffing their caps in fealty—
Even the proscenium's subservient
arch bows and begs a platform for
actors trumpeting loft-aired routines,
voluminous efffusions or, what's worse,
kingly-haired creatures washing
the feet of their inferiors, sudsy
obsequious declamatory eruptions
filled with the rehearsed lava of
bold slaves, the bald brimmings
of an improperly-public humility
(unlike the servant who never spills
his waiting master's entree except
in the pantry when there is no-one
to witness his extravagant remorse)—
All these openly-imploring apertures,
these theme-cut bubblings-up, paeans,
(akin to pale critics' acclamations)
would crack like a laughtrack at
that imposture, that pastiche, applause:
who'd pity these pathetic devotees,
advocates haunted by nothingness,
by that same humanhood to whom
white placecards validate each plate.
Who sat us here? (Athwart this portrait
the descending order of our dinner
ranks auditions more disdain,
every hors d'oeuvre daubed with scorn)—
In our state, our omnipresence,
to which can we aspire? Sometimes
we think: if only there were Someone
somewhere, somehow, though of course
that's impossible: Someone outside
this frame—an absent self, a spectator
vivid at duress, who can feel
the real joy and pain we mime—

who sees the sun setting out there now,
the approach of a nighttime unlike
our curtain: Someone who lacks
the judas window wherein we acolytes
recognize ourselves, the betrayal
portal we have all portrayed so
plausibly it has at last retained us,
replaced us with stainedglass.
(Through which, on rare occasions,
that said Someone fills us with light,
illuminates us.)—Overcome, undone,
we feel ourselves vanish, we dwindle
to a painted panel. We fade, we die.
His stasis renders us too slenderly.
Or is this endless attendance
the promised purgation, the shedding
of every emotion, every weight?
Is it gain, this loss, this usurped,
staged starving, this repast-of-reruns
upon a menu whose full-promised
delicacies remain a manna dream,
backdrop glamour (milk-and-honey)
a feastless Eden, a heaven hunger's
expelled whole from. Why aren't we
at home here, in this plenty, this
supernal supper—why this finicky
desire to avoid the silverware, the knife
paler (because it reflects us) than
the poor fork that renews whose flesh
and encores veins across each dish
until its unction-urged tines impale
spearlike and nail the cacodaemon
that shall huzzah hail our Hostmaster . . .
See: the chair He occupied is empty—
expecting the miracle or bloodcrime
through which all of us must assume

His part, the mummers-meal, the sealed
communion. Bard bread, scene wine,
unyield your transubstantiations:
beyond that superceded throne
lies the utter ubiquity of the known.
And so, viva, bravo, boffo, olé,
so each paraclete's performance moves us.
Cheers! echoes the pledge, promiscuous
each voice ID's the oath. The mic
on the dais quivers, shook by our cry,
sole intercessor of this ceremony.

UNTITLED

I fear my arrow may consider
the target, the bullseye,
merely a toehold.
But to what further can it aspire?

I hope they put a plaque
on the tree Jackson Pollack
crashed his car into,
on which his death is probably no longer visible.

And what about the cloths
Sylvia Plath stuffed
in the door of her kids' room

before gassing herself:
What if I stretched them out on this easel?
What if I painted on them?

COSTARRING OSCAR WILDE AS MADAME SOSOSTRIS

White: white as a tablecloth that moonlights as a bride
For the unborn you—appeared—or a waterfall
Which leans against another waterfall (your hair).
My beeper slave of lost voices barked: *what?*

While the cup that knelt to summer burst; I tried
To garden the fireplace and farm the doormat
But proto-frog-photos of you grew inside me there,
Groping with bare hands of flood my gnarlgargoyle.

Deeper than my beeper you knew; sibyled guesses.
And yet . . . 'misery is proximity.' Oh
The seance was as far as possible tuxedoes.

Aftermath is a mouth. Speaks. Speaks? Yes, but less as
Flesh than what; yak mask for that old fop Apollo?
The god retrieves his gloves
                              and, feigning to go, goes.

TO MYSELF

Poetry
can be
that magic
carpet

which you say
you want,
but only
if you

stand willing
to pull
the rug out

from under
your own
feet, daily.

ALPHABETICAL MORNING

Stabbed by an elephant lens
On a meatless mattress I lie,
(Use a scalpel to trace my future;
The past, a suture) and die.

Spat at as often as the oil
Portrait of a moviestar on
The wall of a Death Row cell I fell
Into an abyss of worn-off

Sculptors' thumbs. Accidentally
Daily I cutted my throat on the
Drinking fountain. How was I

To know there is no justice,
Just a your-honor of trash?
I smile, a total inutile.

Note:
Title: of a painting by Alberto Savinio.

POEMCLONE #4: HIS LIFE, HIS FATE (LAMENT)

Beautiful as a TV tuned to me,
Ending every line with words that end in
The letter z renders him total, final,
Whole. By analogy? Ergo-oh-oh,

How simul/how my epitome's prose. So
Extra-lapsed from time—from time's yawns blending
Our matinal soles (our toll-head of vesper) where
My brain (that scab of bonbons) mimes a dung-

Gone thing as long—as long as this elevator
Of nothingness descends into whose lungs . . .
This down-urge of air, this breathe-me, breathe-me . . .

Then: whenever the xerox cries he dies.
Is it fancy, is it drifty? What's all or null
If I see my teardrops copy my eyes.

UNTURNAROUNDED (MEDUSA SAYS #4)

The way a ballerina boards a gunboat
At twilight in the tropics catches
Its carat out of what a critic watches
A scarecrow paint landscapes through: cuts pans zooms—

As long as we are forced to live in rooms
Having more than one wall our wounds' candies
Will never taste at last born. Tangents apart,
I mean, sightlines aside. Door some more? Therefore

The thermometers we stir our iced drinks with
Fizz with fever, with 'originality';
To focus, one must first empty the lens—

Where—river rumored or swan it's-said or
Moon bruited—my sculptor-scarecrow now bends:
Each snake has hold a chisel: that's handy.

AFTER THE PERSIAN GULF WAR (March–June 1991)

1. Blitzbiz

I was born to dive into a straw, swim through
a straw, emerge from a straw—
Sudden, glistening, the mediabreak
made me drink ice tea in a sandstorm.

Now even the core of a sleepmask digs
in me for the place I love least to go. Ink-length
away, its sky the color of manacles will
hold my toes locked to another's fingers:

count up, with them, the death on them. Memorize
these faces propped against the hearth of an
earthquake daily, pure propitiates. Sweet

cathedral built to pyromania's standards,
Icarus parachutes into the midst
of a cockfight and look! wins his feathers back.

2. The Outremerican Religion

Emerson said I must know it all firsthand.
I can't simply take another's word for it—
no: I must go there, experience it myself.
But in order to go there I need a car,

need gas, need oil. Like Jack Kerouac
I must cross the country incessantly using
whatever-it-takes: like Elizabeth
Bishop I must never stop traveling to see

the world close-up, anti-vicariously, re
my Outremerican masters drawn one by one
down that road, out past that sea, unkenning

the cost, not reckoning the loss of fossil
fuels my ego entails in fulfilling this
me-feel-or-fail, I-go-to-be philosophy.

(Don't stop—
            indulge
                    my need
                            for unmediated

experiential
            direct
                    nonsurrogate
—fuck periphrase!—to

whom the immediacy of
personal hands-on
on-the-spot

on-the-scene
is vis a vis. Is Ism/ Real—
Artless. Autobiographical. Allyouall.)

3. Roadshow (Via Crucis)

Now the Saved the Lost
together must cross

Outremerica . . .
and down that downsome

road, god we're gonesome!
Gas station stasis—?

or 'Moral Crisis'?
Hear our war, our prayer:

Oh Christian Fathers—
Reagan, Bush—give us

a nation fit to
drive children through.

In herds,
with guns at their heads.

4. Garden of the Aediles

It remains beneath the lids to be
seen says memory. Vestige is mostly
an orchestra led by a dowser,
veiled, a water traced in testament,

thirst for it heaps each drop with desert.
False tooth fed into a rifle,
that distance mows us down. Our
lens weighs what, our faith? Outtakes

droughttakes where pillars of smoke
guide more children digging boundaries
whose tourists long to obey

any songbird's prey. High from its wells
they soar, branches scorched in charcoal,
limbs perched upon a pencilsill.

Note:
I can't resist appending just one quote from Our Redeemer Ralph Waldo: "Everything good is on the highway." (But don't forget to bring your Gulf creditcard!)

MINOR POEM

The only response
to a child's grave is
to lie down before it and play dead

SECURITY

If I had a magic carpet I'd keep it
Floating always right in front of me
Perpendicular, like a door.

A SOUTHERN RUN

1. At My Grandparents' Grave, Chokenhole, Alabama

Let me return then, greenly festive,
a sleepwalker on stilts, a water-
lily on crutches. Give me leave, or shade
to smile, to claim: I'm like chafe-artists,

who do stuff to you with their wrists.
Plaintively I will try to rise to mend
your interior fruit vined round my lithe brand
of bracelet therapy. Or is it all lies,

my care, my concern? A drop of rain
might leaf—might root through entire orchards
to find the word that precedes the spade:

one word. The fear of which, if I believe,
I have sworn to stop, to burn cities
for each larva that escapes into love.

2. Disquisition at Knott's Funeral Home, Jelly Neck, Arkansas

Auscultate the boring symptoms of the dead
that heartbeat you do not hear is meat grafted
onto shadows, diagnose these future lives
may vidsnaps and ground zeroes grow on their graves.

Slap in the left hand Damocles' last wig
pinch in the right St. Sebastian's pincushion
scraped from your skin, imagine you ascend
a child's tooth-mussed smile, a cyborg's toe-tag.

Till this resounds solely on what seldom sea
oh net of pores, can you catch a body sheered
laocoon-clear above such wave-dextrous shores.

Assuming one has dredged from the flesh
of the moment himself, has taken the requisite
steps to emerge as me, who am I to be.

3. At My Grandchildren's Grave, Dunceville, Georgia

Will disguising my hemophilia as realism
overcome the humiliation of being,
quote, uninsurable! Like Ellen Barkin in
Siesta, I'm posthumous but make a great smarmpiece

to orifice around with, blasé or various—
Stunt-winged, avant, we grope our precarious
karma, daredevils soaring up actuarial
charts! Oh midnight-ignored spasms, cameo

confessions—here I am, the soul complains,
in hock to meat. And, its co-stars all chorus,
I owe bread a living, of course! Some child's

jump-rhyme, some game. Autism's pious request
to glue my name's lips to mine. No! here comes
a pristine to kiss us; a prim to hug us.

Note:
Siesta—1987 film by Mary Lambert, in which Barkin plays a gregarious ghost.

4. Accidie in Kilborn's Adult Arcade, Cuffs Cliff, Kentucky

So begun-gone, so commence-ended.
A delve away, only sleep is obediant to dawn.
The day bathed in jaunt, cerulean popcorn pouring—
So I beg the alms to interrogate my palm.

Knee-plenty take me. The topsheet teethes on us;
the cunning foreskin heaps up nakedness;
coulda-buddha-beens, nirvana-neverweres.
That table where the room is crowded looking

at photos of itself, that chair; anywhere
our mapping marauders, their cuticle helmets
withheld on high, thrash through ramblethorn bush:
spectrum for time's homonymgram. Thumbthroe?

Often the skull's skill at making masks is
unsurpassed by any dot I subscribe to.

5. At My Grandclone's Grave, Photomyopia, Mississippi

You said that hair was merely the head out of focus
and thus for a male, for me, growing old and bald must
mean entering the picture is leaving it. And yet, here,
when the cemetery grass paints my toenails with smoke I

need you to refute me more the ground I walk on,
not cloud. That uncarpeted core of space is where
there's too much perch to pose for polaroid-deviled scans—
they sun us toward life's Project Face, as if death

is young enough to get I.D. Gee it de-I.Q.'s me
to hear you say that skimming through nulls and skies negatives
the event to wait for a burial that involves

just ourself: see these forehead plod lines, the skull the flesh
which wings washed from me at birth have daubed listless
verdure over, the gaze ending so firmly in lax?

6. After Fainting in Bill's BeautyTique, Mocha Rendezvous,
   Louisiana

Until your cilia refilled me I spilled—
ooze from the wreck of some penicillin pickup,
no hush path closing my aimless course, I was
sipping thighclaps on intermittent maps.

Life, sulk suicide. Pout puke preoccupied.
A dirge-grid doves sieve themselves through.
Cream of my colophon, klieg backwards, how
I peered in at the blowtorch's privacy. Now

I want to weld wings onto my letteropener
if I have a letteropener: the slander
of such truth is the saliva I long to be
mounted by, transphallic-tepid. A noose for

a backpack, I camp beneath the quicken tree.
Source ass, I am a horse brained by its mane.

HITLER SKELETON GOLDPLATED
(FROM TREASURES OF THE C.I.A. MUSEUM,
EDITED BY HILTON KRAMER,
WITH AN INTRODUCTION BY JERZY KOSINSKI.
RANDOM HOUSE/IBM, 1984)

What falls from the drunken pliers of my nose
President-pit pope-rind police-bone
Is all they got on this fucking menu
Always the pure provend of more more more

The piss tease of masterpiece ass
The missionary position is there to catch you
If you drip off that mosquito plaque I guess
Gumming a gifthorse's defectual innocence

The gunfire in the hills is old and I
Am one pile of shit which will never excrete a human
Hey Parliament Congress Politburo

My cock/my KGB has it on lasertape
The moon posing between the horns of a bull
Two hymens touching through milk

THE ENEMY

Like everyone I demand to be
Defended unto the death of
All who defend me, all the
World's people I command to
Roundabout me shield me on
Guard, tall, arm in arms to
Fight off the enemy. My
Theory is if they all stand
Banded together and wall me
Safe, there's no one left to
Be the enemy. Unless I of
Course start attack, snap-
Ping and shattering my fists
On your invincible backs.

OUR CATACOMB'S NEXT MARTYR

The demonic city, the wretchedness of suburbs,
Bodies fished out of rivers, and distress
In the hospitals are also on my list.
(Oh blindfold-anointed night, Nero Nixon nevermore.)

Waiting for dawn to rate the sky X. Love. Love—
The trendsetters yawn over their trendsets—
Hey, Hiroshima: duck! While the fuck of it
Sucks a crucifix stuck in the rat-hole door

Of the secret vault where a Getty gloats
Whole floors of masterpieces, real Mona Lisa and all.
In curtseyland I'll take my stand he screams.

The sound blood makes dripping on their neon
Must of bored the crowd. Facade-trod face of:
Inflect with your name time sours my knees.

Note:
Lines 1-3: "He wrote about the demonic city, the wretchedness of suburbs, bodies fished out of rivers, and distress in the hospitals." —Armin Arnold, writing about George Heym. Lines 9-10: Getty Museum richest in world. (Anyway, most 'masterpieces' in museums are forgeries; the real stuff is sequestered by billionaires.)

MALE MENOPAUSE POEM

How as to lean my non-eon on autumn's roan
Undoing, to smile while the stymies crawl
All over me and the prismatic blindfold
Around my testicles creaks: guess this house

No longer knows which door I am. The window
We were, does it remember its view? You-or-I
Saw so little out there; what future: only
Snatches, catnaps of nightmares yet to come.

Doorknobs worn to doornubs—grey stubble on
Gaunt armpits—lists like that litter this earth.
A lattice of graves greets me or is kind to me;

My hair plowed with parents, their protracted
Smoothings of some poor, tuckablanket bed.
As said each road I find in your face is fled.

CHRISTMAS AT THE ORPHANAGE

But if they'd give us toys and twice the stuff
most parents splurge on the average kid,
orphans, I submit, need more than enough;
in fact, stacks wrapped with our names nearly hid
the tree where sparkling allotments yearly
guaranteed a lack of—what?—family?—

I knew exactly what it was I missed:
(did each boy there feel the same denial?)
to share my pals' tearing open their piles
meant sealing the self, the child that wanted
to scream at all *You stole those gifts from me;*
whose birthday is worth such words? The wish-lists
they'd made us write out in May lay granted
against starred branches. I said I'm sorry.

THE ABSTINENT

The only face I will never find
between my teeth
continues to quote me . . .

[The eyes, built on a ruins
which is the skull, rise.]

THE GOLDEN AGE

is thought to be a confession, won by endless
torture, but which our interrogators must
hate to record—all those old code names, dates,

the standard narrative of sandpaper
throats, even their remorse, fall ignored. Far

away, a late (not lost) messenger stares,
struck by window bargains or is it the gift
of a sudden solicitude: is she going to
lift up her shadow's weight, shift hers
onto it? She knows who bears whom. In

that momentary museum where memory occurs,
more accrue of those torturers' pincers than
lessened fingernails, eyes teased to a pulp,
we beg for closeups. *Ormolus, objets d'art!*
A satyr drains an hourglass with one gulp.

EXCERPTS/VIETNAM

1. Despair

I stick my head into a womb and make faces
at the unborn. I force down their throats
the mating-cries of extinct animals, the traces.
I wait for that, I write filler for suicide-notes.

2. Vietnam in Chicago

Oh it's easy to find Vietnam in Chicago—
we are what's lost (knock at your shadow
to ask the way home from death).

3. Reminder to Nuke the Other Side of the Planet

Upside down in the ground
there is someone who walks
on my soles when I walk.

I'm gonna get that bastard!

MY MOTHER'S LIST OF NAMES

My mother's list of names today I take it in my hand
And I read the places she underlined William and Ann
The others are my brothers and sisters I know
I'm going to see them when I'm fully grown

Yes they're waiting for me to join em and I will
Just over the top of that great big hill
Lies a green valley where their shouts of joy are fellowing
Save all but one can be seen there next a kin

And a link is missing from their ringarosey dance
Think of the names she wrote down not just by chance
When she learned that a baby inside her was growing small
She placed that list inside the family Bible

Then I was born and she died soon after
And I grew up sinful of questions I could not ask her
I did not know that she had left me the answer
Pressed between the holy pages with the happy laughter
Of John, Rudolph, Frank, Arthur, Paul,
Pauline, Martha, Ann, Doris, Susan, you all,

I did not even know you were alive
Till I read the Bible today for the first time in my life

And I found this list of names that might have been my own
You other me's on the bright side of my moon

Mother and Daddy too have joined you in play
And I am coming to complete the circle of your day
I was a lonely child I never understood that you
Were waiting for me to find the truth and know

And I'll make this one promise you want me to:
I'm goin to continue my Bible study
Till I'm back inside the Body
With you

DEPRESSIONISM

Without any necessity to name it or anything,
I remember this bombcrater before it held a garden.
Once I saw children kneel down there to pray for pardon
At an altar on which a little toll-money rolled laughing.

Swift suedes of evening, night's purple peltdown.
I don't have to invoke the past; it's not required.
I'll just settle here stolid like a stopsign repeating
The word I stand for—sit and let my tired feet hang

Over the lip of this pit-deep garden whose intricate
Vines query up at me. Quiet from the town I can hear
Orphans rattling the gravel on their plates and or

Other faux pas I'm under no order to enumerate,—
Jet-lag of angels, a snake, faintings on summer pavements.
This bombfall failed in its intent: having none, I won't.

NUN CLAIMS MOST SNAKES TOO SERIOUS TO MAKE GOOD BOOKMARKS (YOUR SOUL IS A CHOSEN LANDSCAPE)

À la gongs, that await the Emperor's semen
But in vain, I partition silence into rooms
Called poems. Why?—Only Empresses remain—
Why am I needed if seed blown from some

Sunflower comes to land solely on sundials . . .
Yet wig of compass-needles; comet. Soars
—For sync's sake? Like optional hearts, in styles
Singular averse against the opus wall of stars,

Spring safetypins my penis to my navel,
Praying that so fetal a petal shall shrivel still:
A thank-quiet follows; a field-day feeling;

Queen Staypower paints out our scene's see-me's
(Dream-prussic pupils flare, flush with their irises).
Then the sun wonderlands it all a bit, by falling.

Note:
Parenthetical title: "Votre âme est un paysage choisi . . ." —the first line of Verlaine's *Clair de Lune*.

AN OBSOLESCENT AND HIS DEITY (POLYPTYCH)

(for Charles Simic)

Bending over like this to get my hands empty
Rummaging through the white trashcans out back
Of the Patent Office, I find a kind of peace
Here, in this warm-lit alley where no one comes.

For even the lowest know that nothing new
Is going to be thrown out now—no formula,
Never not one blueprint will show up in these
Bright bins, their futures are huge, pristine.

Old alleymouth grabbags my attention at times
I see the world flash by out there, furtive as
The doors of decontamination chambers—

I return to my dull, boring search, foraging
For the feel it gives me of the thing which has
Invented me: that void whose sole idea I was.

VAGUE CONSOLES

This vista often awarded John Ford his rest.
Myself, scenery has a lack of I (emphasis).
And haven't we killed all the Indians yet?
In a stagecoach—made of sagebrush, no doubt—,

I would gauche-out like a tumbleweed at a sockhop.
Yo, watch it roll across the old gym-floor, loboto
Basketball: then, toed by foetid teens, fall,
Slo-mo, as though some flair for the vague consoles—

Oh lips refusing their tongues' rights, bodies
Trying to put down the peaceful demands of
Their genitalia . . . yes everything looks better shot

Through John Wayne's hurt. The sky the way it mattes—
The desert. A lone rider, whose moral I await.
The crotches arranging themselves for death.

Note:
Title: a phrase from Mallarmé's commentary on his *Sonnet en yx*. This poem is perhaps only relevant to those who grew up in the 1940s and 50s watching cowboy movies and going to sockhops.

TO OUTREMERICAN POETS

"The peach-blossom follows the moving water . . .
there is another heaven and earth beyond
the world of men." —Li Po

1.

There's no time left to write poems.
If you will write rallyingcries, yes, do so,
otherwise write poems then throw yourselves on the river to drift
        away.
Li Po's peach-blossom, even if it departs this world, can't help us.
Pound's or Williams' theories on prosody don't meet the cries of
        dying children
(whose death I think is no caesura).
Soon there will be no ideas but in things,
in rubble, in skulls held under the oceans' magnifying-glass,
in screams driven into one lightning-void.
Only you can resurrect the present. People
need your voice to come among them like nakedness,
to fuse them into one marching language in which the word "peace"
        will be said for the last time.
Write slogans, write bread that pounds the table for silence,
write what I can't imagine: words to wake me and all those
who slump over like sapped tombstones when the Generals talk.
The world is not divided into your schools of poetry.
No: there are the destroyers—the Johnsons, Kys, Rusks, Hitlers,
        Francos—then there are those
they want to destroy—lovers, teachers, plows, potatoes:

this is the division. You
are not important. Your black mountains, solitary farms,
LSD trains. Don't forget: you are important.
If you fail, there will be no-one left to say so.
If you succeed, there will also be a great silence. Your names, an
    open
secret in all hearts, no-one will say. But everywhere
they will be finishing the poems you broke away from.

2.

What I mean is: maybe you are the earth's last poets.
Li Po's riverbank poems are far, far out in eternity—
but a nuclear war could blow us that far in an instant:
there's no time left.
Tolstoy's "I would plow."
Plow, plow. But with no-one left to seed, reap,
you write? Oh rocks are
shortlived as us now. But still this BillyBuddworld
blesses its murderers with Spring even as I write this . . .
so I have nowhere else to turn to but you.
Old echoes are useless. Glare
from the fireball this planet will become already makes shadows of
    us.
There's Einstein.—The light
of poems streaking through space, growing younger, younger,
becoming the poet again somewhere? No!
What I mean is. . . .

Notes:
Lines 3-4: Li Po would write a poem while sitting on a riverbank, then lay it on
the water and watch it float away.
Line 6: cummings: "and death i think is no parenthesis."
Line 7: Williams: "No ideas but in things."
Line 30: Tolstoy, out plowing a field one morning, was asked what he'd do if he
knew he would be dead by nightfall. The quote is Tolstoy's answer.

PRISONER

What raw name scrapes and saws at my breath-hatch . . .
This voice wanted always only to soothe, not grate.
And its last noise, that rasp, that deathrale scratch?
—A file, smuggled in to an empty jail cell, too late.

THE GETAWAY

It's 1969—and I'm

All lam: down
These libertysplit streets
U.S.A. I

Throw a measuringtape out, run its length,
Throw again, run,
Throw, run.

FBI KILLS MARTIN LUTHER KING

When this calendar has
undressed will I know, I mean
be able to recognize,
its most naked day—

but to see what was
in what is mistakes time
for its effect—I study
my hand, how
the palm hides in it, slyly,
or like a sullen puddle
refusing reflections—

and my 2-scoops-please blouse—
a passerby's
meander-fall hair—
though the sky's blue is through-outed
with spots of balm, do

they all
praise null but you,
null but them?

THE QUESTION

Far off, demimordial, I hear an epitaph of ears, someone
Collides with a stopwatch, innocent mincemeats rise steaming and
Sporadic laughter, cardoors going slammed. Then, static-ier voices,
Through blood jettisoned by mimes statues reminisce, reveal how
They subsist on glimpsed nubility, personal-touches in crowds who
Traipse past. In rooms where you heard the sound of a teardrop
Striking the bloodhound surface of perfume which sat in a
Washbasin, chipped fake porcelain, who poured it in that? in
Those rooms (where you were so strangely audient!), others, like
Me, are listening. Outside, in the city, the minstrelshow
Pollution (which paints us all in 'blackface') continues, corny
And racist, sexist, lampoonist . . . humanist? Ashes watered
By hell, kisses skimmed from doveflight, cream from silk, what-
Ever rises, curdled, from depths as fraught with else as these,
Far off. . . . Yet I would encourage your traits your tricks individual
Of speech, you crowds who gape on as those rooms all rush toward
One room, whose doors part now like a mouth pried in cry
Silently, stifled by its openness. Will my voice receive me,
Will my cries still have me? will not be the question there.

MORE BEST JOKES OF THE DELPHIC ORACLE

"Eigentlich spricht die Sprache"
—Heidegger

I vow to live always at trash point: to
Waste my past talking about the weather
In mirrors, how they cloud or is it clear
With no certain referent to that what was

Forecast. Like Snow White's dust-draped stepmother
I smile up at the dictionary whispering
My favorite definition, down at the stove my
Worst recipe. The endproduct in me

Agrees. It and I are one in this blither
And, I believe, we echo something endless,
Eine global vocal. Will those lips ever

Repent this recorded message. Lips
That remain a mere testimonial
To the inchworm's socialization progress.

Note:
Epigraph: "Speech is language made literal" or "Talk talks till it's true" or "Tongue is the only word the tongue says for real" or something like that. ("Language is Delphi."—Novalis)

ART OR THE CARESSES OR THE SPHINX (CASTRATION ENVY #36)

The Lord Peter Mumsey of Thebes, that yummy
Oedi-poo dick, advises me, It's no use. To
Detectify a guilty party will
Soil the purity of our respective plagues.

Like a silo filled with silhouettes of sigh
I reply. My smarm/your frissonpassion
To be eliminated from the world's
Verticalities are more of what photons do

To Phaëtons. Therefore, if that obliteracy
Our face slash esperanto saliva
Trace or clue is left to sift through but this

Issuey stuff, whoa, who's to blame, us?! So I whore
Is for sure and if death occurs, facile
Excel. 'What's named between the knees' 's not me.

Note:
Title (excluding the parenthesis): of a work by Khnopff. Line 14: I can't recall
where this quote comes from, or if in fact it is a quote.

ANCIENT MEASURES

As much as someone could plow in one day
They called an acre;
As much as a person could die in one instant
A lifetime—

POEM TO POETRY

Poetry,
you are an electric,
a magic, field—like the space
between a sleepwalker's outheld arms!

SLEEP

We brush the other, invisible moon.
Its caves come out and carry us inside.

WHERE

are the arrows that

have bandages instead

of feathers at

their ends

(CASTRATION ENVY #21) DOES THE SWORDSWALLOWER SHIT PLOWSHARES?

Sure: the more me, the more morituri.
Mine duels his hand some scroll of manliness,
Whose downfall almost dolored us. Though
Soon, up the brain tanks, gracias oozed.

The hair is a cohort of this. The hair,
Or the beard, a creditcard used as a napkin,
Swiping off a chin. "My adam's apple's agog!"
Quote: Exclude before you begin the male

Because it is vile. "The heart in common
Is the heart withheld," another recommends;
Hey here comes my favorite human-razed future.

Xerox of course a tapeworm lost inside
A hunchback, I squirm manfully on.
Deep in the direction known as thumbsdown.

Note:
Line 1: Morituri te salutamus—we who are about to die salute you: the gladia-
tors' obeisance to the Roman emperor. Line 8–9: Exclude before you begin etc.:
a pun on Mallarmé's "Exclus-en si tu commences / Le réel parce que vil".

NO ANDROGYNE IS AN ARCHIPELAGO

The butterfingers things that hold us know
To plunk the gut strings of your suturous
Lobotomy lyre—but if it is to pore
Iota'd digits through a wall with no elses

In it I do not. Who scans test tubes for
The fatal ripple of my beauty finds
That long meant mirror has fled in error since
In their clone alphabet seems I'm z:

This crystalball bilge/ouch mosaic of
Out of touch omens will not tune true too as
My leavetaking leaking everywhere sees

A 'puter oh! inventory zeroes.
Why try to guess which one comes last? Just zoom
Your monitor. The past the gist of it gets us.

LESSON

Even if the mountain I climbed
Proved to be just a duncecap really,
It was only on gaining its peak
That that knowledge reached me.

SAVE AS: SALVATION

Somewhere is the software to ID all
The snowflakes falling in this storm, but there
Ain't enough RAM crammed in my brain to call
Them forth by name, each crystal character
Putered and programmed, made to have a soul:
And even if I compelled the power
To inscribe them here as equals, in whole
Terms, I would not permit such an error.

But which is which, cries Ms. Ubiq-Unique.
We're not formatted for whiteout. And when
The screen of your vision freezes in flurries
And the core of this word blizzard hurries
To melt again, to find itself again,
Won't mine be the sign these syllables seek?

SELF-PORTRAIT OF THE POET AS HYENA

Kindly deferrer to lions,
Late flocks of vultures, packs of winds.

Last to destroy the lost, discreet,
A shy, toothpick aristocrat.

Servile, even, leaning over
Droves of bones who disdain such care,

Who in their marrow preen and bear
Huge swarms of self, a hubris herd.

Is that why he laughs—why he finds
Joy in these humiliations,

These measured modesties that mass
And make him eat his words at last?

How strange it is to stay astride
This prey, to taste its pride of pride.

COCTEAU'S STARS IMPORTUNED

Cocteau's stars are bored by the love
of a sort of wince-animal,
who's failed throughout his life no less
to stretch a pimple into a profile.

Pipes ache to anchor in those teeth—
a sail, a horsestall, a fireplace
all beg to go backdrop, to gaze
agonized at your white spines.

Pruned against mirror, I imagine
laundering such muse, laving such sheets:
Oh simul-semen! kill this puny poem,

whose publication has been timed
to coincide with the release of
my latest film, *Fetish Sans Flesh*.

TEMPTROUSSEAU

The clock is dressed in drag, I mean it wears
space instead of its own proper aspect—
but if it wore *time*, would it disappear—
isn't visibility an effect

of transvestism, that shield/pastime whose
crosscausal aim unmasks the eye: must you
assume the costume of the other to
be here, to present the sense with an ess . . .

Narcissus saw his guise decked out all ruse,
but if there were none, what would our true clothes
consist of, our rig rags, our regalia—

Whose dapper element dons us: Einstein's
continuum—or Flaubert's confidence
that come the same, the Bovary c'est Moi?

CELEBRATION

The conversation-pit is filled to the level
Of the floor with the soil of former parties here—
Crushed cigarettes, napkins, all kinds of cocktail swill—
We stand at its edge, grinning, wondering who's there:

Is there some version of us lost down in that dross.
Such a Pompeii probably took years of soirees.
Where's the carpet to cover it—dense, bottomless,
It makes the livingroom around it seem empty.

And why get superstitious—why greet our fellow
Guest from way across this trashhold—since we must know
Its surface could bear our most intimate meetings.

Oh, somewhere the host is winking working elbows,
Showing no embarrassment—but here we have grown
Sober over the grave of what greater gatherings.

PLAZA DE LOCO

It's high tide in the hero
The floodgates fail the heart cowers
Blood of his deeds drowns the town square
Above it all this statue towers

And as the captain of a sinking ship
The instant the waves reach his toes
Snaps to attention it stands
Commanding some former pose

The inscription on which is blurred
Hey what is that word
What does his crumbling mad pedestal say

To find my way to you is
To not find your way to you
And therefore is not to find the way

LAPSE POETICA

Smashing the elixir of life while
shouting "From now on this is my life!"
may not be the best manner
to ensure progress, I know. One

never dips apes into human navels
in order to baptize angels,
even if those navels are absolutely
as we say, brimming. Filled with

the water, the essential eau de vie—
Blink, blink, my teardrops blurted,
do you think we enjoy chewing
that sphinx's loudest eyelash?!

If just one of them cum comes true, I'll let
each new you-pseudonym name me its.

(PLEA, HOPELESS, SUB VOCE)

Murderous the gist
of their paws condemns
us all to die of applause:
in this circus minimus
even Coriolanus must
nurse and gnaw and showcase
his scars when the next
closeup comes.
                    (*But not my poems—!*)

CLARINET

It's like a scissors
popsicle I don't know to
whether jump back
or lick

TWO EPIGRAMS FROM A NOTEBOOK DATED 1984

1. [The ageing epigrammatarian]

Youth's engine
of thumbs revs
and purrs—

Oh:
I am all
fingers now.

2. [Plus ça change . . .]

When young
I was attracted to what they call
Older women.

Older now
I am attracted to what they call
Old women.

I SHOULD HOPE SO

Next year when this book is
pulped and the pulp recycled to
print your Collected Poems, will I
still be here still writing this?

HOLY SHIT

Gosh golly Galway Kinnell's pig is holy and I
Am holy too and so are you and gee if I could only
Find the name of the right saint to throw in here they
Would print this next to his in all their anthology.

Note:
After Kinnell's "Saint Francis and the Sow."

CASTRATION ENVY #12 (COLLECTED PORTRAITS OF THE MARCHESA CASATI)

The knifefighter's mouth on my cancelled flesh
While, mutinous, tincan-incommunicato, I
—Or in that psycho syringe my face, all
The thawed camel of my eyes, the ball

Point pen pickling in my anus writes poem:
Trapped by titular star-wince, is it sky
I always escape from, to make the lam my home . . . hmm?
Unless my blood—like some more intimate

Form of ivy cover it—blond abattoir
Where a loincloth contemplates emptiness
Or less. Slash-wounds they should rename me for.

My gordian sex axed solves one puzzle though
I hesitate still, to give this portrait
A sign. Pool of saliva under the mistletoe?

Note:
The Marchesa Casati "was painted by fifty or more artists" (Philippe Julian). It would make a fascinating exhibit to see all of these portraits hung, one after another, upon a nail protruding from my forehead.

RESUMED PLEA

To pick up where I left off
at birth,
as I was about to say before
being interrupted by
the midwife,
my parents,
my teachers,
my commanding officer,
my employers,
my various wives/children etc.,
my physician,
one or two astrologers,
and the undertaker:

"Free me or worship me!"

THE HEROES CROWD EACH OTHER AT THE GATE

But this cryptic impulse to eclipse a map
While voiceovers avail one's profile or
The blindfolds floating to the ground smile
The vegetation shiver a little

Light has not accustomed swimmingpools to this
Glitter and illiterates with gold records know
And all our next door to door neighbors the Nukes
Family who play charades to remember

Each other's names they feel it hie vie die
Across that oversuffice of knife their life
Santa's reindeer sneer down from the sky as

Guiding your foot with my hand to its mark
My face I reflect of how this world which
Does not consist of more you's than you does

Note:
Title: a phrase by Abel Gance; as quoted in the screenplay for *Hitler: A Film from Germany.*

THE PRESIDENT OF DESCENT (NEOCOLONIALISM #16)

'Insomnia, so I shot a few natives.'
Still, dawn has its palliatives; the cast sky
Lobs bullseye haloes; bolts of overview below
That pit whose voice timbers my spine: but why

Dis-niche this idol/this fiction called me? Which
A fluke, a fault, a streak of makeup down
A mirror where a stroke victim leaned to kiss—
Oh say the not right-out-of-it, say know.

Tongue: lightswitch of the body. Head: ha.
I'm serious! Every fable's a linear
Of topplings. And what falls first? Neck second

—I guess. Torso—torso off of groin goes—
And so on downwards—downwards—thighs knees et al.
The feet are a final ruins; the toes, shards.

Note:
Neocolonialism: Outremer, Europe's first attempt to create a "USA", fell after 2 or 3 centuries, overrun by 'the natives'. . . xerox for us? Ah the comminution of this latter Crusade; me, crumb.

FEAR OF DOMESTICITY

(after reading Plath and Sexton)

Eyelashes did their job:
they lengthened the afternoon,
like a dress-hem.

Then that night the hem began to rise, in stages
revealing
scenes from my shameful life.

—Those calves
up which the hem reproachfully rasped,
catching,
lingering over whatever scene

(the higher the younger) arose
on those calves
knees, thighs, those
woman-segments

or were they mine—
I hid my eyes.
I wouldn't attend to
the walls either

endless walls, slowly
basted
with suicide.

The eyelashes did their job.
But I, who could neither sew
nor cook groped and groped those long legs
stubborn, afraid to look.

THE WISHINGWELL STANZAS

Oracle whose hollow
catalogs each word I swallow,
I wish my birth had been false, I wish
the pregnancy which bled me was kitsch.

Nothing the pupil paints on our
eye easel will equal your
entry in non-entity,
whose unpaginate genitalia I
am one lack-me of.
May I try or is it type
to man-ingest the woman-digest of this?

Only a fishhook can play Hamlet adequately—
bright as skin pinned to a candle,
go dangle down a well, chapel
by inversion; the bells toll,
the toads flick my gnat-name home.

Oldest lodge and once as I was,
bring me, lightning for ballast,
the memory of a boy crossing
a creekbed, a ditch, look,
in which he steps on a snake:
I felt it shift, beneath my shoe,
felt tremor after tremor go
through my length, lure up muck
so far back. Its meander meat
realigned the path I meant to
take, my heel hung there
caught in the quickest loss
of ground, my footing was gone
from the moment and I poised
on flesh that refuted my own—
orator atop a trapdoor.

The ponderous sack of semen slice off:
sever all, soil it to the ground—
solve with blood the gordianhood, praise
this surface sacrifice, curse it and dance
over dying coils on virile instep,
stomp this lance that lacks true sibilance,
there, there, contrary penis! the drum and
the tambour of the Mother
the earthquake have spoke—

in *Catullus LXIII*
the faultline runs
from clit to anus, but can
an equator debate
itself—are they castrate
enough, these Attis strata—
at Delphi does my vein begin, then, or end?

Her hallowed handled echoes call
to me this cisternship, this landslide
water, oh Pythoness, oh cult-consumed womb;
let some aquarium of seeps accept each
of my pennies, my worthless wishes—
each treasure I offer the Goddess
mercifully confirms my emptiness.

TANKATOWN

This island has
Been discovered by a great explorer,
But fortunately,
News of the discovery
Has not reached here yet.

POEM!

Shh, you'll wake up the stains on my bedsheets.

28-LINE POEM

All it takes is Laura Riding's riding-
crop across my butt, and I'm off:
Git-up horsie she cries astride me as
I crash sweetly onto the carpet.

Boredom what an esthetic,
cleansing the days—
I laud the vintage of my toothpick.

Small-husband to the floor,
my foot stoops in dance,
in courtship intervals.

Putting their clothes on afterwards
the lovers are surprised
at how empty
the buttonholes seem.

Like one of those catatonics who go
nuts and run around screaming if they happen to
overhear the name of their first therapist,
dare I listen for my "accidental" words most?

Hypercraze puzzles, they come conundrum
contorting themselves in the tongue's regress,
as if each birth expressed what must be repressed. . . .
Jinxed from the start-fate, sphinxed by origin—

against its heart-riddles, what pre-oedipal
will pile up high my years' eclipsedness—
wall that has no Rec Room in it, no niche-all,
no refuge from the familiar other? Act One

finds our face mano a mano the Goddess.
I adore men with momentary nostrils She says.

BEST WAY TO KEEP YOUR ANKLES AWAKE? SNAKE SHOELACES

Only a scratch, but its bandage patrols the walled
city, assuming this mystic furrow has taught such
fangs repose. Past suburbs skilled with ash, past
evaporated sculpture, blindpond bodies. Or is it

like maples, learning their craft of syrup—years
of drop on drop, step by step—have we, life after
life, a soul-spoor gradually maximizing its sugar?
Or is Nirvana bitter—a clockmarked zero, a pine-

needle's grudging eye. A void, propped up by sim-
plicity. Where someone exhausted by the justice
of his meals pauses in the street, the proof his
feet make gathers, gravity snatching to earth all

sweets. Even sprinters, on their starting-blocks,
hold hands. Love? A sideways noise, a tidings via
toe-graphologists, rumor as raw as cold as saliva
crawling on the floor of a crematorium, straw used

to sip frogsweat from sleeping lilypads. More?—
Mourners, televidilevitated. Birth, its strength
of recap. The yacht of yet, the boat of but, have
never saved us from sinking in dreams where the dead

must keep their day jobs: imagine going on working
like a compass on the thrust-out palm of some lost
Victorian's corpse near the North Pole: think of how
tired it is by now sticking to the point, the poem.

RECAP

It was that kind of day
The kind that goes through you
like a skewer but is okay as long
as there's someone beside you
waiting ready to lick the skewer
when it emerges from you

IDEAL ESTHETIC

I only keep this voice to give to anything afraid of me

GOODBYE

If you are still alive when you read this,
close your eyes. I am
under their lids, growing black.

DEATH

Going to sleep, I cross my hands on my chest.
They will place my hands like this.
It will look as though I am flying into myself.

SAY WHEN

I write poems that consist of nothing
but the word attentionspan
attentionspan
fills all the pages of all my books
of course it's boring for you
to read the same word
printed over and over again
I agree it's a waste
of time and patience in fact
I know you probably won't even
read past the first thousand or so
that's okay I am not hurt by the fact
that you never read my poems all
the way through because (and get this)
wherever you do stop reading
wherever you toss me aside
is where I triumph
is where I impose upon you
the term for that limit which
you have haughtily and
eternally tried to impose upon me
right there
wherever you stop
will be the word for that stop
the true word the word
made deed as we say in the trade
you will have reached your attentionspan

and I will have put it there
waiting for you
writing it over and over for you
sitting in this crummy room day after day
gloating over this victory
over your usual tyranny
over me

THE FINAL WORD

Our farewells lack the plausibility of our departures.

ACKNOWLEDGMENTS PAGE

This is where I'm supposed to thank the editors of the journals where these poems first appeared, but I think everything in this book was rejected at least six times by various mags, and indeed the majority of the poems here never did achieve the honor of periodical publication.

—And of the few poems that did make it into some crummy little mag, not one was ever selected by annual "best of the year" anthols like *Borestone Mountain*, *Yearbook of Magazine Verse*, *Pushcart*, or *Lehman's Best American*. . . .

If they didn't think the poems in this book were any good, why are you reading it?

ABOUT THE AUTHOR

Bill Knott is an assistant professor at Emerson College in Boston.

INDEX

BOA EDITIONS, LTD.
AMERICAN POETS CONTINUUM SERIES

Vol. 1   *The Fuhrer Bunker: A Cycle of Poems in Progress*
W. D. Snodgrass

Vol. 2   *She*
M. L. Rosenthal

Vol. 3   *Living With Distance*
Ralph J. Mills, Jr.

Vol. 4   *Not Just Any Death*
Michael Waters

Vol. 5   *That Was Then: New and Selected Poems*
Isabella Gardner

Vol. 6   *Things That Happen Where There Aren't Any People*
William Stafford

Vol. 7   *The Bridge of Change: Poems 1974–1980*
John Logan

Vol. 8   *Signatures*
Joseph Stroud

Vol. 9   *People Live Here: Selected Poems 1949–1983*
Louis Simpson

Vol. 10   *Yin*
Carolyn Kizer

Vol. 11   *Duhamel: Ideas of Order in Little Canada*
Bill Tremblay

Vol. 12   *Seeing It Was So*
Anthony Piccione

Vol. 13   *Hyam Plutzik: The Collected Poems*

Vol. 14   *Good Woman: Poems and a Memoir 1969–1980*
Lucille Clifton

Vol. 15   *Next: New Poems*
Lucille Clifton

Vol. 16   *Roxa: Voices of the Culver Family*
William B. Patrick

Vol. 17   *John Logan: The Collected Poems*

Vol. 18   *Isabella Gardner: The Collected Poems*

Vol. 19   *The Sunken Lightship*
Peter Makuck

Vol. 20   *The City in Which I Love You*
Li-Young Lee

Vol. 21   *Quilting: Poems 1987–1990*
Lucille Clifton

Vol. 22   *John Logan: The Collected Fiction*

Vol. 23   *Shenandoah and Other Verse Plays*
Delmore Schwartz

Vol. 24   *Nobody Lives on Arthur Godfrey Boulevard*
Gerald Costanzo

Vol. 25   *The Book of Names: New and Selected Poems*
Barton Sutter

Vol. 26   *Each in His Season*
W. D. Snodgrass

Vol. 27   *Wordworks: Poems Selected and New*
Richard Kostelanetz

Vol. 28   *What We Carry*
Dorianne Laux

Vol. 29   *Red Suitcase*
Naomi Shihab Nye

Vol. 30   *Song*
Brigit Pegeen Kelly

Vol. 31   *The Fuehrer Bunker: The Complete Cycle*
W. D. Snodgrass

Vol. 32   *For the Kingdom*
Anthony Piccione

Vol. 33   *The Quicken Tree*
Bill Knott

Vol. 34   *These Upraised Hands*
William B. Patrick

Vol. 35   *Crazy Horse in Stillness*
William Heyen

COLOPHON

The publication of this book was made possible,
in part, by the special support of the following individuals:

Richard Garth & Mimi Hwang,
Dane & Judy Gordon, Robert & Willy Hursh,
Archie & Pat Kutz, Jennifer & Craig Litt,
Boo Poulin, Alva & Irene Royston,
Andrea & Paul Rubery, H. Allen Spencer,
Pat & Michael Wilder,
and In Memory of George R. Parsons, Jr.

This book was set in Goudy fonts
by Richard Foerster, York Beach, Maine.
The cover was designed by Daphne Poulin-Stofer.
Manufacturing was by McNaughton & Gunn,
Saline, Michigan.